Bringing Baby Home

An Owner's Manual for First-Time Parents

Laura Zahn

Down to Earth Publications

St. Paul, Minnesota

To Jay
without whom my interest in this topic
would not have been necessary or possible

with thanks to Jim
without whom Jay would not have been possible

Published by Down to Earth Publications, Inc.
1032 W. Montana Ave.
St. Paul, MN 55117

Distributed to the book trade by **Independent Publishers Group, 1-800-888-4741**

ISBN 0-939301-91-1

This book is intended to provide information and support to two-parent couples of full-term, healthy babies delivered by health care professionals in a hospital setting. Because all babies are different, not all information is suitable for every baby. The author is not a doctor and this book is not intended to replace a doctor's advice. If you have any questions at any time about your baby or its care, do not hesitate to contact a health care professional. The author, publishers and distributors cannot be held responsible and disclaim any liability directly or indirectly arising from the use of this book.

Library of Congress Cataloging in Publication Data

Zahn, Laura, 1957-
Bringing Baby Home - An Owner's Manual for First-Time Parents/by Laura Zahn
p. cm.
Includes index

1. Infants   (Newborn) - Care. 2. Child rearing. 3. Parent and infant.
I. Title.

RJ253.Z24 1993   649.1'22

Cover by Joy Dey, Deer Path Studio, Duluth, Minn.
Text illustrations by Mark Jirsa, Mounds View, Minn.
Photos by Laura Zahn, St. Paul, Minn.

Printed on recycled paper

Printed in the USA on 50% recycled, acid-free paper

For single-copy orders by phone with a V/MC, call 1-800-585-6211. By mail, send a check for $12.95, ppd., to Down to Earth Publications, 1032 W. Montana Ave., St. Paul, MN 55117.

Many people helped research or review this book. Special thanks to the Childbirth Education Association (CEA) of St. Paul, for support and information, especially Judy Berven, Nan Miller and Lynn Arnold there. Also special thanks to Beth Davis and Colleen Rusch.

Many thanks, too, to Tyler, Rita and Ronnie Salone, Emily Rose Walsh, Amy Hadiaris and Jim Walsh, Janet and Jim Paces, Sherryl Livingston and Jim Lundy, Terry Wulf, Marilyn Calver and Tim Parker, Julie Larson, Jane and Tom Cleland, LoAnn and Bill Mockler, Peggy Rader and Bob von Sternberg, Lisa Roy and Erasmus Meinerts, Collette Crumb, Kathy and Chris Hull, Linda Johnson and Clare Marshall.

Special help was appreciated from Linda Doyle, Diane Pfeifer, Nancy Edwards, Donna Montgomery, Jill Sundberg and Gary Gustavson, Kathy O'Neill, Kristina Ford, Sharry Buckner, Linda Sonna, Roberta, Colleen and Bonnie at the Nursing Mothers Counsel, Jan Wenig, Sylvia Morse, Sharry, Nancy, Tom and Pearl at the Hungry Mind, the American Academy of Pediatrics, Jan Nelson, Peg Meier and the talented Joy Dey and Mark Jirsa.

Contents:

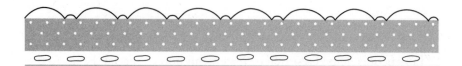

It just gets better and better

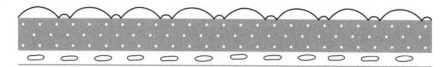

Babies can be scary. They can seem uncontrolled, irrational. Who knows what makes them tick. They cry for no apparent reason. If you make a funny face at one that is not your own, it might laugh, it might cry. There's no telling about baby senses of humor.

Newborn babies can be doubly scary, maybe triply scary. For people who have not been around them — and that's a lot of people, since new parents don't turn brand new babies over to sitters or inexperienced relatives — they really are a mystery. Compared to older children and babies, their eyes seem not to focus, their arms and legs jerk around independently of any purposeful motion, their cries can be high-pitched and instantly hysterical. At the same time, they are so tiny and fragile-looking that it seems merely picking them up could break them in two.

In the "old days" (say, in the '50s and before), new parents used to live close to — or with — their own parents, so newborn care knowledge was easily passed on from generation to generation. When that baby cried at 2 a.m., the parents *and* a grandmother or great aunt might very well have been there to answer the need. When the baby got colic, the grandparents or other relatives babysat for an hour or two to give the parents a needed break.

Today, families are spread out around the country, or world, and new parents may find themselves in a town thousands of miles from the nearest relative, people who are bound by blood to help you with that new member of the family tree (friends have no such obligation). Oh, sure, you can call, or you might get one to come and stay when you first come home from the hospital. But it's not like having Grandma around the corner.

If you are an "older" parent, you may have developed a parenting inferiority complex. Perhaps your family considered you weird for "waiting so long." Perhaps they might have indicated that, oh sure, you can hold down a big-time job, but you couldn't change a diaper if your life depended on it. Nevermind that until you had your own baby, there was no need, and certainly no interest, in knowing how to change a diaper. It's not something you normally question, like why is the sky blue, or something practical to know, like how to change a tire.

My guess is, those reasons — that newborn babies are really scary, that Grandma doesn't live here anymore and that you feel unprepared to bring a baby home — are why you are reading this book. You're not interested, yet, in common toilet training problems that bigger books cover. You don't want to hurt The Fragile One by doing something "wrong." You're afraid it'll cry and cry and you won't know how to get it to stop.

And, many parents will agree, you are right to worry that the first month or so at home probably is not going to be a picnic.

Most likely, mom will be tired from labor and delivery (downright laid-up if you had a cesarean delivery). Your baby will be eating maybe every two hours, 24 hours a day, so you will be sleep-deprived. If mom is nursing, it may not be going so well the first couple weeks. New moms have a bloody discharge and often have hemorrhoids, healing episiotomy stitches, mood swings, sore breasts and a body that's still wearing maternity clothes. Your purpose in life has changed from perhaps holding a responsible job in the stimulating company of other responsible, skilled adults to rushing at the first peep of this seven or eight-pound bundle to make sure the bundle is full, dry, clean and warm (but not too warm) — from the office scoop to baby poop, as it were.

You may feel as though you are not able to leave the house because the baby is asleep, or the baby is awake, and you have to feed it in 20 minutes, or maybe two hours, and you have to put it in the car seat, and put the car seat in the car, and take the car seat out of the car, and haul along enough supplies to break the back of the men who carried their supplies to the Klondike gold fields. You may not have time or energy to say anything to your spouse except, "Hand me that clean diaper — now!" Your personal hygiene may be reduced to a 10-second shower during a baby nap ("Gee, what if he wakes up hungry and I'm in the shower? Or he wakes up *choking* and I'm in the shower?").

Then, put yourself in your newborn's booties. He or she spent nine months in the perfect environment — consistently warm, continuously fed, always listening to mom's reassuring heartbeat. The birth was a major deal. Now there's light and cold and loud noises and hard surfaces and gravity, and food isn't readily accessible and work is needed to obtain it. And this child does not have the skills or ability to communicate his or her displeasure, confusion or frustration except by screaming. Your baby is more than a little freaked out during the first month.

But a funny thing happened to this new mother about two or three months out. I started telling people, "Gee, motherhood is a lot more fun than I thought it would be." And they responded, almost verbatim — and these were people who didn't know each other, mind you — "and it just gets better and better."

"And it just gets better and better." It seems to be universally understood — though not admitted — that the first month can be really awful, both for new parents and for the new baby, and things get easier after that.

So you have dished out about the price of baby's first booties for this book, and I thank you for that, and applaud your good sense (or that of the thoughtful people who bought it for your gift). But now that you have done so, I am going to tell you: there are no right or wrong ways of doing things. Of course, there are some safer ones. For example, when cleaning during a diaper change, don't wipe from the rectum forward into the urethra, spreading fecal coliform bacteria (especially easy to do on baby girls). And make sure that baby's skin is dry before putting on a clean diaper, because wetness can lead to diaper rash. But beyond that, the right way to change a diaper is the way it works for you.

In addition to there being no right or wrong ways, there are no perfect solutions. What works for one baby may not work at all for yours, or only work sometimes. Your baby may adore the sound of the vacuum cleaner, even fall asleep to it. Your neighbor's baby may scream every time it's turned on. I apologize if you find this book is ambiguous, not specific enough. I tried to provide some meaty information, though someone, somewhere will probably disagree with everything that's more than wishy-washy. At the same time, I tried to give ideas to try, things you may not have thought of yourself. Please remember this book is supposed to give the basics for only the first month. If you want intricate detail about things like how to tell spit-up from vomit, buy Dr. Spock. (Seriously. He's helpful.)

Each baby truly is an individual, with his or her own system, his or her own personality, his or her own preferences. This is Zahn's Law: What can defy the baby books, will. If newborns typically go through 12 diapers a day, yours will go through 20. If orthodontic pacifiers or nipples are supposed to be "better," yours won't like them. If the cord is supposed to fall off in 10 days, it will take four weeks. If babies usually sleep two hours at a time, yours will sleep 30 minutes. And so on, with every other aspect of the baby's life. You get the idea. You will get to know your baby's likes and dislikes quickly, within a month or two, and then he or she will change, and all of a sudden the orthodontic pacifier is just fine, thank you.

That may sound tremendously difficult to manage. But most of the time, so what? There's often nothing to worry about if your baby is "different" than what The Books say. Of course, you don't know that, so you call the pediatrician's office and are put through to a nurse, who seems to be reading out of the same baby care books you are. That's one reason a common-sense, easy-going, easily-accessible doctor — or one with a "phone nurse" who is that way — can be a Godsend.

Thank goodness for parent intuition. At the two-week check-up, one set of parents was told that feeding their baby more often than every two hours would set up snacking habits that would lead to obesity and be with him all his life. (That very well may be, and perhaps the doctor was over-cautious about bottlefed babies. But they didn't believe habits could be formed at age 2 weeks. Making him cry was worse, and they continued to feed him when he was hungry, two hours or not.) A nursing mother was told the reason her newborn had green stools was because she was eating green vegetables and she should quit eating them. (She quit seeing that pediatrician; baby poop often is green — or brown, or yellow.) It's important to trust your heart and your gut — you know more than you think you do.

There often is considerable disagreement in the medical community, and favored practices tend to change. For example, parents used to be told to let their babies cry if they woke up in the morning an hour early; it'd teach those little devils patience or something. Now the thinking is more "on demand," to go ahead and feed, change, hold or rock a baby when he or she wants it; it'll teach trust, that "my needs will be taken care of." It may also mean, eventually, that baby will cry less when hungry, because baby knows there's no reason to scream — he or she *will* get fed. But that may take awhile, perhaps several months. In the first month, you can expect that when your baby says, "Jump," you say, "How high, my little baby, my slavemaster?"

Let this book be a help, then, when your slavemaster is calling, or, hopefully, before then. Once you have some confidence in "how to do things," or at least one or two ways to do things, and some knowledge about basic baby care, you and your intuition will do fine. Honest.

And it just gets better and better.

Laura Zahn
St. Paul, Minnesota

A new baby, a new life

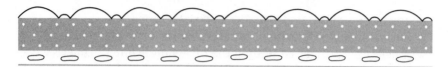

As a first-time parent, you know that your life will be very different when you bring that newborn baby home to live with you. But how, exactly? How does a newborn spend the day?

Newborns *are* different from older babies, and many first-time parents have never had experience with brand-new babies.

Obviously, newborns can't go very far on their own power. That's a blessing, because you don't have to worry about them crawling into the bathroom and drinking poison toilet-bowl cleaner the first day home from the hospital. You have some time to grow with them and adjust to their new capabilities.

What do newborns do all day?

If you've had friends or relatives with newborns, you may have noticed they sort of lock themselves indoors that first week or two, or even month, and you might not know why. Of course, they're tired.

But *why* are they tired, other than continued recovery from labor and delivery and getting up two or three or four times every night? Here's a run down on how much time caring for a new baby takes.

Sleeping

Your baby may sleep from 15 minutes to 6 hours at a time.

THE GOOD NEWS is, newborns may sleep 16 hours out of 24 (they may be exhausted from delivery and sleep a lot the first two or three days). The bad news is, sleeping may be in short stretches. Your baby may sleep from 15 minutes to six hours at a time. She or he may fall asleep and snooze six or seven times a day.

Babies have deep (non-Rapid Eye Movement) sleep in which they may sleep through loud noises and being handled. They also have several light (Rapid Eye Movement) naps, in which you can see eye movements under the lids or even slightly open eyes, body twitches and even sucking attempts or grimaces. Babies may be easily awakened in the REM stage. A complete cycle of REM and non-REM sleep takes about 50 minutes.

But when you hear people say, "Newborns are so easy—all they do is sleep," don't believe it. They also eat, cry, dirty their diapers and look around, taking in their new world.

EXPECT TO CHANGE a diaper six to twelve times a day, possibly more. Some experts say going through 20 cloth diapers (cloth ones hold less urine than disposables) a day is not unheard of...

Because diapers leak, or because you may be taking the baby outside, an outfit change may be required at the same time as a diaper change. Diaper/ outfit changes take about 15 minutes at first. If you're talking about bundling those tiny hands and feet into winter outfits, however, it takes amazingly long. (In other words, that can be 2.5 hours of your day.)

Diaper/ clothing changes

Expect to change a diaper six to twelve times a day, possibly more.

How to dress a newborn

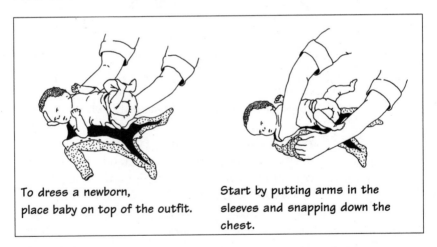

To dress a newborn, place baby on top of the outfit.

Start by putting arms in the sleeves and snapping down the chest.

NEWBORNS MAY EAT every one to four hours, for 20 or more minutes at a time. (Pediatricians sometimes note babies don't *need* to eat more frequently than every two hours, but try telling that to your crying newborn.) That may take up eight hours of your day.

Feeding

Crying

Yours may only whimper for the few minutes it takes to fix the problem.

"CRYING IS NORMAL," you can keep telling yourself. "It is one of my baby's ways of communicating." He or she may "communicate" for three hours, off and on, on a good day, some researchers say. But that would be only if you had a very fussy baby. Yours may only whimper for the few minutes it takes to fix the problem.

The baby may develop colic at age 2 or 3 weeks. Colic is generally fussy crying every day at about the same time of day, and the fussing/crying may start at 5 p.m. or so and go to midnight (or it may be at another time of the day). *[See section on Crying, p. 17]*

Chores

Gee, what did you do all day?

DON'T FORGET that you'll be spending time preparing baby bottles, if you don't breastfeed or are supplementing the feedings with bottles. Baby laundry needs to be done separately from the rest of the family's, probably every other day. Home-laundered diapers should be done at least every other day, washed separately from everything else.

Woe be to the spouse who has returned to a job outside the home, then comes home to an exhausted spouse and says, "Gee, what did you do all day?" Double woe be to the spouse who comes home late (that caregiver may have been counting the minutes until the return of the support and relief person). And triple woe be to the parent who dares to carp, "How come the house is such a mess?" (A jury of new stay-at-home parents might rule it was justifiable homicide.)

Where do they do it?

Sleep

The baby may feel more secure swaddled in a blanket.

BABIES EVENTUALLY SLEEP in cribs (and may use that crib for three or more years). But after nine months in a secure, warm womb, a big crib for a little baby may not be close enough for comfort. The baby may feel more secure swaddled in a blanket or touching the side of the "bed." Many parents buy a bassinet or cradle, which often come waist-high, the right height for picking up your bundle of joy about 2,000 times a day, and with wheels.

Many a youngster has started life at home sleep-

This baby started life at home in a padded laundry basket. He slept on his side, with padding at his back to keep him from rolling over onto his back. (The ruler is for scale; kids, don't try this at home.)

ing in a washed and padded laundry basket, dresser drawer or similar-sized heavy box. Make sure the padding is very firm so baby can't sink in it and suffocate. Likewise, never use "Moses baskets" or other items with collapsible sides.

Whether to put the bassinet in the parents' room or the baby's room at night is up to the new parents.

Some parents believe having the baby in their room will save steps during the inevitable night-time wake ups. Others believe parents need their sleep, and privacy, and that they may be more likely not to rush to the baby who is not really wide awake and in need of attention if the baby is in its own room. Some parents find their newborn is a noisy roommate, snorting and sneezing and full of little baby moans, and that one or both parents wake up with baby's every little murmur.

Some parents find their newborn is a noisy roommate.

Another debate rages over having the baby actually sleep in the parents' bed. Surely all children crawl into bed with their parents at one time or another for comfort. It can be convenient for breastfeeding moms. Families in other cultures sleep this way. Parents and the new baby snuggling together can be an intimate experience. Some say sleeping with parents builds security in babies, and that it's natural and healthy.

On the down side, sleeping with your baby may "invade" the marital bed, keeping parents from enjoying better sleep and needed privacy.

The American Academy of Pediatrics and the Sleep Products Safety Council have run ads in parenting magazines warning "never leave an infant on an adult mattress. Infants can suffocate if trapped between the mattress and the wall, bed frame, footboard or headboard. Never sleep in the same bed as an infant. The infant can become wedged between your body and the mattress and suffocate." Also, infants have suffocated sleeping on their stomachs on adult or youth waterbeds. For those safety reasons, the U.S. Consumer Product Safety Commission recommends a crib with a tight-fitting mattress.

As an alternative to the parents' bed, some parents keep a mattress on the floor right next to their bed. When baby needs comforting or feeding, one parent can slip out of bed and cuddle there with the baby for awhile. Sleeping there with the baby, however, doesn't relieve the above safety concerns.

Another option is to split shifts—one parent gets the bedroom, the other gets the guest room with the baby. Parents can do it either in nightly shifts, before and after 3 a.m., for instance, ensuring one parent a half night's sleep. Or they can trade baby duty every other night. (That won't work if mom is breastfeeding, however, and has to be up with baby.)

Some of these decisions, of course, depend on whether you have a separate room for baby and how much you can or want to spend on nursery items. Remember that baby is too small to care whether it has a fancy bassinet, and that bassinet will be outgrown in perhaps two or three months, but a crib will be used for a long time. On the other hand, a bassinet

Another option is to split shifts.

is more easily moved than a crib, so baby in a bassinet may be able to "hang out" in a room with a parent.

ANOTHER DEBATE exists about whether babies who can't yet turn themselves over (or even raise their heads) should be put to bed on their stomachs or their backs.

One theory is that babies sleeping on their stomachs can't turn their heads to avoid being suffocated by a mattress pad, pillow or other soft object. Recent research suggests that babies at risk for SIDS (Sudden Infant Death Syndrome) may be more likely to stop breathing if placed on their stomachs, basically because they may not be getting enough oxygen and are incapable of turning or lifting their heads to do so.

Another theory is that babies who spit up a lot and who sleep on their backs can suffocate on their own spit-up.

As a result, many parents choose to have newborns sleep on their side with padding behind their back and perhaps in front of their tummy, but well away from their face (this position also is good until the umbilical cord stump falls off because rubbing during stomach sleeping can irritate the skin around the drying cord).

The best solution may be talking with your own doctor about your baby's needs.

AS SUCCESSFULLY NURSING moms will testify, babies (and moms) can do this anywhere. During the first month, though, it's nice to have a private or quiet place for this. Whether breast or bottle-fed, a rocking chair is helpful, especially to quiet an infant a little before feeding. Grab a pillow for your lap, place baby on it, prop up your feet on a footstool, then offer breast or bottle and lots of lovey baby talk and eye contact. (Moms may want a pillow behind their shoulder or arm, as well.)

A POPULAR DAYTIME SEAT for infants is a sort-of baby version of the recliner-lounger. This is a padded baby-carrier seat (not a car seat) on a metal or plastic

Sleep position

Many parents choose to have newborns sleep on their side.

The best solution may be talking with your own doctor about your baby's needs.

Eat

Whether breast or bottle-fed, a rocking chair is helpful.

Wake

frame. Brightly-colored cloth is slung over the frame, with a seat or crotch snaps, and with a matching head-roll pad for use during the first month or so. Usually there is a bar above the seat with baby toys, which can

At age three weeks, Tyler enjoys lounging about the house in this seat. He can't yet play with the attached toys (and parents may want to remove them for ease of slipping baby in and out). He's wearing baby socks on his hands to keep him from scratching his face.

be removed. Baby is strapped in and reclined and can see what's going on.

Caution: Don't use this on a table with babies who are becoming mobile or could kick their way out or over to the edge of the table. Don't leave a baby in it on a bed, as beds are not stable. The safest place for placing these is on the floor. Make sure the padding or covering is not so thick to cause suffocating, if it were to flap over baby's mouth and nose. And *never* use these as car seats; they are not approved for car safety.

Babies also can be toted around the house in a front-pack or sling (they thrive on body contact), wheeled in their bassinets, placed in their car seats, or set in the middle of the floor on a bright blanket.

What a newborn can do

At birth or within the first weeks, healthy newborns usually:

- See objects 8-12 inches away (the distance from breast or bottle to mom's or dad's face)
- Can hear and may move their heads and eyes to hear or see something of interest, or turn their heads if their breathing is blocked (but sometimes not enough to prevent suffocation - see Safety First chapter)
- Can recognize their parents' voices
- Can taste and smell and have shown preferences for their own mother's milk and dislikes for strong, offensive odors
- Can pull back when pinched or pricked
- Can yawn and sneeze
- Have a "startle reflex," in which the arms and legs may shoot out or their body may stiffen when startled by a loud noise or other stimulation
- Have a "rooting reflex," in which touching the baby's lips gets him or her to open its mouth for feeding, perhaps smacking lips, sucking and breathing excitedly
- Have a protective reflex in which their tongues push out any object in their mouths (such as pacifiers, which you may want to stay in!). This reflex is designed to protect them against choking
- Have a "stepping reflex" if held upright and a "crawling reflex," in which they appear to sort-of crawl when placed on their stomach
- Have a "grasping reflex," in which they tighten their little hands

around a finger or other object
- Have a "righting reflex," in which when pulled up by the arms, they can pull their head up, despite a floppy neck
- Get a big kick out of faces, their own or other people's, and may be able to imitate expressions a few days after birth
- Prefer the contrast of black-and-white patterns, especially the edges and in the shapes of bullseyes, diagonal stripes, faces or checkerboards

What a newborn *can't do*

Of course, *your* baby will be exceptional, so you can skip this section. But if you want to know what is usually too much to expect of other, more average babies one month or younger, they cannot or do not:

- Smile on purpose (this takes about six weeks, though parents often swear it's sooner)
- See very far away (you'll notice as baby's eyes begin to focus further away)
- Lift head up (maybe a bit by end of month, but little neck control yet)
- Sit alone when put down in sitting position (at about 5-6 months age)
- Eat any solids, and will choke if given them (feeding solids sometimes starts at about 4 or 5 months)
- Drool (drooling may start at about 3 months)
- Have teeth (rarely a newborn is born with a tooth, but most infants get first teeth at 4-12 months)
- Hold, pick up or grab objects (by 6 months, though, you may be wishing for a baby straitjacket at the grocery store)
- Beg, whine and cry for heavily advertised toys (thank your lucky stars)
- Watch TV (that will start shockingly soon. "Wheel of Fortune," with its noisy wheel, bells, buzzers and flashing colors, was interesting to this author's child, she is ashamed to admit, at about age 5 months. {Honestly.} At 10 months, he loved to clap along. {Really.} At the tender age of 1, he knew which station it was on, commanded the remote control, and he could chant, "Come on, big money." We bought stock in King World. {OK, that's an exaggeration, but only slight.}).

The first year really is incredible. What is now to you an unfocused, uncontrolled, helpless newborn, your genius child will be able to, at age 1, walk, talk, feed itself, eat everything you do except Szechuan beef, drink from a cup, sleep through the night, poke the dog's eyes out, stick fingers in the electrical outlets, give hugs and kisses, pick his/her nose, pick your nose, and see the ice cream truck coming a mile away.

How to pick up a baby

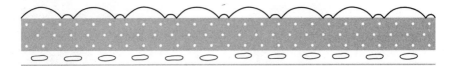

Newborns love to be held, carried, stroked, cuddled and cooed at. Fortunately, new parents usually love it, too. It's hard to overdo it on the "lovey stuff," especially during the first month.

But the first few times you pick up your newborn might be a bit scary or intimidating. They seem tiny and fragile. Fortunately, it doesn't take much practice to learn how to pick up and carry your baby.

ONE WAY to lift a baby lying on his or her back: Scoop one hand under the baby's neck/head. Support the neck with the three "end" fingers; spread your thumb and forefinger to go under and around the back and sides of the baby's head. (See photo, next page.) Place your other hand under the baby's body, then lift both hands together, bringing the baby in close to your body right away. Bring the "head hand" up to your shoulder, cuddling the baby in on your chest. **Provide support**

Because newborns' neck muscles are not very strong, perhaps the most important handling aspect is to keep a hand under their necks, cradling the back of the head. Other than that, don't toss a one-month-old in the air—in fact, be careful *not* to shake or jolt a young baby, as brain damage or death can result.

But do hold and cuddle them. Carry them right-side-up nearly any way that's comfortable for both of you, or with the baby's tummy resting on your arm as in a "football hold." **Do hold and cuddle them**

"Front packs" are popular for newborns because the baby rests in roughly the same position as in the womb, hearing the parent's heartbeat and feeling body warmth (though don't wear them too low, or it will hurt parents' backs and swing the baby too much). The baby may also like being closely held, as

Neck support is crucial in holding and carrying a newborn. Dad's bottom three fingers support baby's neck, while his forefinger and thumb cradle the head.

The above position leaves one hand free. (With good deep-knee bends, you'll be amazed at what you can do with one hand.)

when he or she is swaddled. At the same time, mom's or dad's hands are free. Make sure the neck of a newborn is supported. Read and follow the manufacturer's directions.

Commercial baby slings also are another option, and are favored by many nursing moms. Baby is "worn" on the side. Again, make sure the neck of a newborn is supported, and read and follow the manufacturer's directions.

Crying

A crying newborn can be one of the most frustrating and frightening experiences for new parents, and parents often worry about how they'll handle crying even before the baby is born.

It's important to remember crying is normal, and that it's the only way a baby has to communicate. In fact, you don't want a baby *not* to cry, because then it couldn't tell you that it needs your help. But crying is not pleasant. Your dislike of the crying—and your response to get up and do something about it—is how it's supposed to work.

To comfort or not to comfort?

It's AMAZING anyone ever recommended letting a newborn "cry it out." Parental instinct is to be bothered by the crying so parents will attend to their child. Besides, babies that are left to cry often work themselves into more of a snit, making it harder to calm them or tell what's wrong.

Nowadays, the conventional wisdom is that it's impossible to "spoil" an infant by attending to its every cry. In fact, doing so may make baby less likely to cry more (we've all seen—and heard—the toddlers who *yell* at their parents—and everyone else—in order to get them to just listen.). Young babies aren't able to manipulate situations, so there's no way you can spoil them by attending to their needs. In fact, *not* doing so would tell them no one cares about attending to their needs, a message parents don't want to send.

It's impossible to "spoil" an infant by attending to its every cry

Crying Checklist

When crying starts, it's most likely because of:
- hunger (though if it hasn't been about two hours since feeding, you can usually rule this one out, but you might try feeding anyway)
- diaper needs changing

- gas, rash, too hot or cold, or something else producing discomfort
- over-tired or over-stimulated
- bored
- scared, perhaps by a loud noise or unfamiliar person
- in need of being picked up for closeness and comfort
- in pain from a diaper pin or too-tight diaper or elastic band.

So, when the crying starts, run down the above checklist and make sure the baby's needs are met and there's no apparent injury.

Many times, the baby will calm simply by:
- picking the baby up, holding it close to your body in a soft curve, and walking with it or rocking it
- holding it in a front carrier next to mom's or dad's heartbeat (some say babies that are "worn" frequently this way may cry less overall)
- talking in a soothing, calming voice, and/or
- giving it a finger, its own hand or a pacifier to suck.

Other calming techniques:
- Swaddling. Wrap the baby tightly in a receiving blanket, with or without hands available for sucking (sucking its hand may calm the baby in itself). Sometimes the closeness is comforting, much like the womb. The feeling of flailing arms and legs may be like being lost in space.

  To swaddle, put the baby's head on one corner of the blanket. Wrap one corner over the baby and tuck it under the baby's opposite side. Bring the end up and tuck it under the baby's "open" side. Wrap the remaining corner of the blanket over the baby and tuck it into a fold somewhere. (It's sort of like folding the American flag...you might ask the nurses to teach you this before you leave the hospital.)

- Music. A tape of comforting lullabies or special soothing womb-like sounds and heartbeats can be purchased in baby departments, baby specialty stores, some toy stores and baby catalogs. Your own singing is cheaper and may work just as well. Don't forget trying the radio.
- Noise. This might not seem all that different from "music," depending on your singing voice. But "noise" means what's sometimes called "white noise," that steady drone of something that might irritate adults, but magically lulls babies to sleep.

  Turn the vacuum cleaner on near the baby (or put the baby in a front-pack carrier while you vacuum). The vibration and consistent noise comforts many babies.

  The hum of the exhaust fan over the kitchen stove often works. A noisy room fan or air conditioner could have the same effect.

  Combine noise with other techniques, such as swaddling. Or turn on a noisy fan while rocking a swaddled baby.

  A car ride might help, and you don't need to take the muffler off. Just the vibration and hum is sometimes sufficient.
- Massage. Entire books, videos and classes are available on this subject, and many parents find babies respond to gentle massage of arms, legs, chest, back and head. Even without formal training, try rubbing backs or stomachs, which may ease gas pains, while holding the baby or while baby (or you and the baby together) are in the bathtub (remember's babies whose umbilical cords haven't fallen off yet shouldn't take tub baths).
- Motion. How were fussy children raised just a generation ago, when those wind-up swings weren't yet invented? Lots of car rides, apparently. (And before the car?)

19

Swings, by the way, can be used by babies less than a month old, either in a cradle or a seat. Especially for the cradle, make sure the baby is not rolling back and forth with every swing. For the seat, check to see the head is held upright and cradled by a rolled towel or special support pillow. And use the safety belt.

Young babies have a tendency to flop forward, sideways or slink down in the swing seat; *never* leave the baby in the swing unattended, even though it's tempting to do so (hence the swing's slang name, "Neglecto-matic.")

Other motion that seems to work is just walking or putting the baby in a stroller or its car seat and heading outside (the motion or the

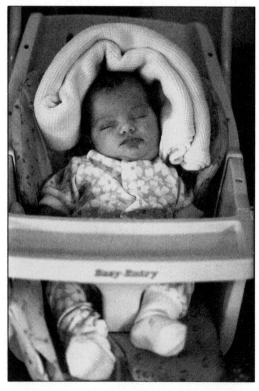

Emily's head is cradled with a rolled towel for extra neck support in the swing.

fresh air or the change of scenery, or all of the above, often helps. A change of scenery helps *you,* too.).

A change of scenery helps you, too

Same with the spin cycle on the washer. Put the washer lid down, of course. Then strap the baby in a car seat or lounge seat and place the seat on top of the washer lid. *Hold onto the seat,* and run the washer through a spin cycle. *Never* try this without holding onto the seat with both hands *the entire time.* Of course, if baby cries more or harder, quit this and cuddle!

Note that babies who like quiet, soft lights and lullabies may not like motion as a calming technique. For others, only bouncing and rhythm works.

- Warmth. Try feeding a bottle of warm water, placing the baby tummy-down on a hot water bottle filled with warm water and covered with a towel or baby blanket, or giving the baby a warm bath, if baby is old enough for a tub bath. (Never use an electric heating pad.) Of course, if it's 90 degrees and humid, opt for a cool sponge bath, instead.

Try to pick one comfort measure and stick with it for 10 or 15 minutes. Then add another method if the first doesn't work. Switching methods every few seconds or minutes can overstimulate babies, when what they really need is time to wind down.

Try to pick one comfort measure and stick with it for 10 or 15 minutes

KNOWING THE DIFFERENCE between a newborn communicating discomfort by crying and communicating real sickness or injury by crying is tricky and frustrating.

Discomfort or Sickness?

Health care professionals say they'd rather field telephone calls early in an illness or "silly questions" than have a parent wait and then try to deal with more severe symptoms or illness. If you feel intimidated or afraid to contact your doctor, get a new doctor.

Watch the child, take his or her temperature and

write down all symptoms and questions you have. (Keep the pad and pen near the phone to write down the answers, too.)

When to call the doctor

Here are some guidelines:

- The short course is to call the doctor if the baby's rectal temperature is 101 or over *(see section on how to take a rectal temperature, p. 83),* and/or if there is a change in behavior or personality (loss of appetite, change in color or breathing habits, unusually quiet, fussy, etc.). *You know your baby best, and you know more than you think you do, so trust your instincts about whether your baby is sick. If you don't feel "right" about something, call the doctor's office. Gut feelings count!*

For a newborn, the longer version is to **call the doctor right away if:**

- The baby just looks sick, perhaps limp or unusually quiet.
- There's a change in breathing (of course, dial 911 if the baby stops breathing or is having trouble), appetite or energy level.
- Diaper rash appears, or any skin rash or blotches that don't appear to be normal scratches or mosquito bites.
- The baby vomits (more projectile than "spit up" after feeding), loses appetite or can't keep anything down. Check for blood or bile (which appears green) in the vomit or if it has an unusual odor. Does the child vomit when coughing?
- Diarrhea occurs, especially if there is blood or pus. Keep track of the color and frequency of the stools, as well as consistency. But don't wait to call the doctor while you're counting blotto'd diapers. *[See the "Is It Diarrhea?" section in the Elimination chapter, p.58.]*
- The baby cries when moved or seems to be in pain.

- Unconsolable crying, probably not related to colic *(see crying and colic, in this chapter)*.
- Eyes are less bright.
- The baby has fallen or been dropped or bumped and there's swelling or redness or a bruise.
- Yellow skin tone or yellowish whites of the eyes, probably indicating jaundice, appear.

WHEN THERE SEEMS to be no reason for continued crying, check to see if:

- All the usual remedies won't work and the baby just seems "fussy"?
- The baby is two or three weeks old or older?
- Crying usually begins about 5 p.m. and may go to midnight (or, even worse, is continuous all day)?

If you've answered "yes!" to two or three of those questions, it may be the time when babies develop colic.

Unconsolable crying

GOOD QUESTION. Short answer: No one agrees. There are many definitions, many alleged causes, and no sure cures. (That's why there are entire books written on this subject, too.)

For our purposes, colic is that "thing" that turns a normally happy baby into someone who cries or fusses, almost non-stop, for more than three hours a day, often in the evening, for no apparent reason. It may "set in" at two or three weeks, peak at about six weeks, and end at about 12 weeks. During that time, parents are severely tested and often feel like they are failures.

Some health care professionals insist "true colic" is when screaming is even more severe and goes on nearly all day and all night.

But there's no agreement on what causes this or what cures it.

Sometimes babies pull their legs up, as though cramped by gas, or they burp or pass gas. For years, the recommendation was to change to formula, chang-

What is "colic"?

There are many definitions, many alleged causes, and no sure cures

ing your regular formula, having breastfeeding moms change their diets, or trying pasteurized goat milk.

Mothers often were unjustly blamed—they were too anxious, they didn't have enough or the "right" milk, they were eating the wrong diet. Allergies and urinary tract infections also have been labeled as causes.

One explanation may be that a young baby's central nervous system is just so immature that, after being stimulated all day, he or she simply blows up in the evening. Crying lets off pressure. When the child is about three months old, she or he is more able to process all the action going on in her or his world, and doesn't need to "depressurize."

Whatever the reason, no one's come up with the magic medicine or method to stop it.

Caring for the colicky baby

IF YOU HAVE a colicky or fussy baby, you may want to check with your pediatrician to determine that there is no illness or injury, or something otherwise unusual, such as an ear or bladder infection or irritating diaper rash.

Then, try the above calming techniques.

- Try only one technique for 15-20 minutes, then give the baby 15-20 minutes "down time" in bed. More than 20 minutes, or trying several calming techniques, may just get the baby more "wound up."
- Let the baby cry during the 15-20 minute "down times." This may be hard and seem cruel. But sometimes babies do let off enough steam and cry themselves to sleep, and there really isn't anything you can do to get them to stop crying. (If you can't wait 20 minutes, set the timer for 10 minutes and go in after that. Ten minutes can seem like forever...)
- Ask other parents and store personnel what has worked for them or shoppers they know. Sometimes there are new products that may be worth a try. For example, a crib shaker that approxi-

mates a 55-mile-per-hour car ride has worked for some babies.

- If it really is stomach gas or milk intolerance, some over-the-counter antacids now are available for infants. Check with your pediatrician before trying one.

Don't expect that what works one time will work every time, or even that you'll find any technique that works, period.

Consider handing the baby over to an understanding relative or friend or babysitter for an hour or more at a time. Eight weeks of this crying, every night, could wear even Mother Theresa down. You'll do better with it if you get away from it periodically.

Don't take it personally. (Repeat that to yourself about every 10 minutes.)

Don't take it personally

Crybabies - Coping with Colic: What to Do When Baby Won't Stop Crying by Marc Weissbluth, M.D. (Arbor House Publishing Co.);

Infant Colic - What It Is and What You Can Do About It by Christopher Farrran (Scribners);

The Fussy Baby - How to Bring Out the Best In Your High-Need Child by William Sears, M.D. (Penguin Books/Signet).

Additional resources

DON'T BE SURPRISED to find new moms weepy after the birth, usually for a week, but sometimes for up to six weeks. It's raging hormones.

Weepiness can be compounded by lack of sleep, anxiety over parenting, not feeling so great after the delivery, an unexpected outcome of pregnancy or grieving over a difficult birth, difficulty breastfeeding, and adjustments to the end of pregnancy and new roles as a parent/family. It's no wonder many a new mom has said, "If I have this beautiful baby and am supposed to be so happy, why I am so miserable?"

Most doctors don't prescribe anything except time to get through this period.

If, however, you become severely depressed—

Crying Mom

"If I have this beautiful baby and am supposed to be so happy, why I am so miserable?"

perhaps you don't want to eat, can't get out of bed, feel out of control, have suicidal thoughts or you want to leave or hurt the baby—call your obstetrician's office right away and tell them you have severe post-partum depression and need help immediately.

If you don't get a supportive response, call a community mental health help-line and ask about where to find help for post-partum depression, or contact the Depression After Delivery Support Group, 215-295-3994, for a local chapter, or contact Parents Anonymous (in the yellow pages under "mental health", or 1-800-421-0353; 213-410-9732). Many larger clinics and hospitals now offer support groups, too. Dads may need to prompt the new mom to seek help, or do so for her, if she's so depressed she can't help herself.

The first month or two may be very difficult

In addition to hormonal concerns, recognize that the first month (or two or three, depending on the baby and parents and their situation) may be very difficult. You may be tired, you may not feel well yet, you may have a baby who is difficult to calm. You may not fall in love with the baby right away, you may not be getting emotional support or physical help from the baby's father, or you may feel trapped in your house, far away from your former life and career.

It's important to get help with the baby and/or around the house from someone. Tell the baby's dad, a friend or a relative that you need help (most folks are glad to be asked, honest) and be specific ("I need a good dinner cooked and the dishes done and the baby watched while I nap or get a shower.").

Get out of the house, if you can, because a change of scenery can do wonders for the psyche. (The baby probably can go, too, but don't feel guilty about leaving baby at home for awhile with someone else.).

Crying Dad

THIS IS A BIG EVENT for a new dad, too, though his feelings or physical exhaustion may be overlooked with the attention on the new baby and new mom.

Physically, if dad was present during a long labor

and then ran off to make phone calls, he may be really tired. If he's rooming in with mom and baby, he's probably not getting much more sleep than they are.

Emotionally, many new fathers feel overwhelmed and awed

Emotionally, many new fathers feel overwhelmed and awed by the experience of labor and delivery (or depressed if they missed it). Sometimes they feel left out of a special closeness between mom and baby, especially if mom is breastfeeding. Sometimes they feel a heavy burden of responsibility to "take care of" this new family, financially and otherwise.

A change in sexual feelings, or confusion about them, after coaching labor and seeing breastfeeding, is not uncommon. Sex may not resume for a long time, and it may be different when it does. Stories about time of resumption of sex range from the one about the woman who became pregnant the first week after delivery to the couple who didn't have sex again for two years. (Don't feel badly if you're closer to the second couple.)

A new-parent support group can be helpful to fathers. Often these groups will have specific topics of discussion, with experts brought in, at each meeting. Suggest topics of particular interest to you.

Give yourself some time to adjust to being the dad (more than a couple weeks...perhaps several months or a year). But if issues linger or cause problems, consider short-term professional counseling as a way to sort through your changing role and feelings. Even if you have others with which to discuss or compare experiences, a good counselor can do more than listen and say, "Yah, that happened to Jerry, too. Bummer." He or she can suggest techniques or bring up specific ideas for working through issues, with or without your partner.

Pacifiers

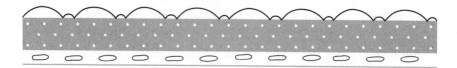

Whether babies should be comforted by a synthetically manufactured "plug," rather than comfort themselves or have a caregiver attend to their needs, is a matter of debate.

Surely parents should find out what's bothering the baby before just stuffing in the pacifier *(see crying checklist in the "Crying" chapter)*. Indeed, in some cases it's the parents, not the baby, who become addicted to the pacifier since it's easier to "give him the bink" than find out what's wrong. Sometimes, however, a pacifier that quiets a crying baby is a godsend. While many babies can and will suck on their hand or fingers to comfort themselves, it may take several weeks before they can actually get their hand to mouth.

Sometimes a pacifier that quiets a crying baby is a godsend

Sucking is necessary for babies (and it may last less than a year). The sucking urge ensures a baby will eat. Many babies get enough satisfaction at the breast or bottle. For these babies, use of a pacifier may provide so much satisfaction that they prefer not to nurse. Others need to suck more and will suck on their hands, parents' fingers, pacifiers or anything that they're able to pop in their mouths. Sometimes, only a pacifier seems to quiet an otherwise attended-to baby.

If you opt for pacifier use

- Buy ones labeled "orthodontic" as they have a special shape best for tongue or palate development. (However, if your child doesn't like these, or any other type, don't worry. Some kids just don't like pacifiers, or won't until they're older. And your baby won't be malformed because he or she used a traditional-shaped pacifier.) You may be able to find special "newborn size" pacifiers, as well.
- Buy silicone, rather than latex/rubber, since

they last longer and are less likely to break off and choke the baby. Also, they can be washed in the dishwasher. (But if your baby has rubber bottle nipples, he or she may prefer rubber pacifiers.)

Some kids just don't like pacifiers, or won't until they're older.

- Buy ones with air holes around the guard or shield around the nipple, so air can circulate and skin won't get irritated by saliva. *The guard should be too big to fit in the baby's mouth and should have ventilation holes so the baby could breathe if it did get in there, anyhow.*
- Clean a new pacifier before use, and test it by pulling on it to make sure no parts tear away (they can cause choking). Test older pacifiers often, too.

Also:
- Never use a homemade pacifier (it won't meet safety standards)
- Never tie the pacifier around the baby's neck or to a cord (baby could strangle)
- Never dip the pacifier in honey (it may cause botulism) or other substances such as alcohol, corn syrup or milk (which could lead to tooth decay or gum disease).
- To get the baby to take it, "tease" their cheek or lip with the pacifier's nipple, as you would to get the baby to take the breast or bottle. It may need to be rubbed on the roof of baby's mouth or held in the baby's mouth for a few seconds before the baby catches on and sucks readily.

Feeding
"Into and out of the mouths of babes"

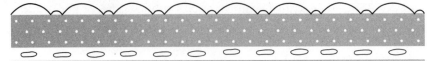

Babies usually don't start eating "solid" foods until they are about four months old, so it's either breast, bottle or both until then.

Never give a young baby cow's milk. It has too much protein and some minerals, too little vitamins and iron, and is too hard on the baby's kidneys and digestive system. Babies should not be switched from breastmilk or formula to whole cow's milk until they are 12 months old or older.

Breast or bottle?

Oh, boy, is this a touchy subject

OH, BOY, is this a touchy subject. It seems no mother is neutral about it, and every mother has strong feelings about whichever method(s) she used. Some mothers are almost crusaders. But because there's so much misinformation and emotion surrounding the subject, this author chose to include this section, but may regret it later!

Nearly every pregnant woman has heard stories from mothers who found breastfeeding such a blissful experience they could have done it all day, or had so much milk and loved to nurse so much they gladly nursed fussy babies who were not their own. Other women said it hurt so badly that they had tears running down their cheeks every time their baby nursed.

It may be hard to decide to continue to breastfeed until that first baby is born and the process has been tried for a few weeks. Experts say moms can expect ups and downs and may want to commit to a trial period of a couple weeks. Some say it takes up to three months to establish a comfortable nursing routine. According to one study by a formula manufacturer, 70 percent of breastfed babies in the U.S. are weaned by the time they are 3-months-old—just when nursing problems should smooth out.

There is little disagreement that breastmilk is best.

However, if something physical or emotional makes the experience very unpleasant for mom, many health care providers agree that babies can sense the tension and resentment, and could be better off with positive bottlefeeding experiences than negative breastfeeding.

While breastfeeding used to be a rather private subject, it's rarely so these days. Friends, relatives and neighbors will ask whether you are breastfeeding or bottlefeeding, why you chose that method and how it's going.

Chances are good that you, the reader, are a formula-fed baby (or were fed on what passed for formula in those days). After all, not so long ago— just one generation—nearly every mother took advantage of newly available formula, often wrongly believing it superior to breastmilk.

Today, the tide has turned and new moms often feel pressured to breastfeed. Breastmilk is considered the perfect food for baby (and what kind of mother would deny her child that?). Formula companies have suffered bad reputations. Women have been told nearly all of them can breastfeed "if they just want to."

Still, bottlefeeding isn't all bad. Many babies are bottlefed (including nearly all adopted babies) and they aren't necessarily sickly, obese, unfulfilled or unbonded to their mothers, nor are their mothers necessarily emotionally distant from their babies. The bad press given formula companies usually came when companies convinced women in developing countries, where formula was diluted or mixed with contaminated water, that bottlefeeding was better than breastfeeding. (The content of formula, by the way, has improved since the mix-your-own concoctions in the '50s.)

But whatever the reason, moms who choose one method over another, or who switch methods, shouldn't feel guilty. As one wise midwife advised: "There's more to mothering than whether to breast- or bottlefeed." You'll have other things to concern yourself with that first month.

Moms who choose one method over another, or who switch methods, shouldn't feel guilty

31

What you do is really no one else's business. Your doctor, midwife, pediatrician or other health care provider should support you either way (as should your spouse, family and friends, in an ideal world!).

Breastfeeding

ENTIRE BOOKS, videos and classes are conducted on this subject, which can't be replicated here. The information below touches on issues which may come up in the first month home with baby, a time when most mothers are not working full-time outside the home and may want to try breastfeeding.

Information and support

BREASTFEEDING doesn't just come naturally—some instruction, and a lot of support, is helpful. Note that weaning, supplementing with a bottle or solid food, teething and other issues may eventually arise after that first month, so seek out more information if you choose to breastfeed.

You may begin breastfeeding in the delivery room. Some research shows that the baby who nurses in the first hour or so after delivery may do better nursing in the long-run than babies who dropped off to sleep and were fed sugar-water four or five hours later. (Also, mom's milk may come in faster and with fewer problems.) However, breastfeeding can be started anytime for several days after birth. Babies who are delivered by cesarean section, for instance, and may not nurse for hours or even a day or two after birth usually do fine at breastfeeding.

If help is not offered, ask the nursing staff while in the hospital to make sure the baby is positioned correctly, and to show you alternative ways to hold the baby while feeding. Ask if the hospital or doctor's office has a "lactation consultant" who has specialized training, and may even be available to come to your home. It's important to get off to a good start.

The La Leche League says it "is a non-profit organization dedicated to supporting breastfeeding worldwide through education, mother-to-mother help, and a network of 8,000 accredited leaders in 46 countries" and that "after 35 years of helping mothers breastfeed their babies, there is no question too big or too small for us to handle." From 9 a.m. to 3 p.m. Central time, Monday through Friday, an accredited "leader" answers breastfeeding questions at 1-800-LA LECHE. The organization also publishes a catalog selling several books on breastfeeding (and other parenting topics). Call 708-451-1891 for the catalog.

The Nursing Mothers Counsel is a non-profit organization dedicated to provide "information, support and encouragement to breastfeeding women," so they may enjoy a successful breastfeeding relationship with their baby. Trained counselors offer a one-to-one phone contact with a woman before and after her delivery. The Counsel will support the mother in whatever she chooses and focus on positive aspects of mothering and nursing. Headquarters are at P.O. Box 50063, Palo Alto, CA 94303. Call 415-591-6688 to get phone numbers of regional chapters.

Advantages of breastfeeding

THERE'S LITTLE DISAGREEMENT that breastmilk is the best food for baby. It is nutritionally balanced and passes along some disease- and allergy-resistance. Some studies have shown IQ scores are higher in children who were fed breastmilk. Formula manufacturers have not been able to duplicate mother's milk.

There's little disagreement that breastmilk is the best food for baby

Other advantages may include: it's inexpensive; it's offered at the "right" temperature; it's quicker than preparing bottles, especially appreciated during night feedings; baby's stools are not offensive in smell; it can be beneficial to the mother to help her uterus contract and return to its normal size; a pleasant breastfeeding experience can help a mother and baby bond; lochia (the discharge from the uterus after birth) may not flow as long; some research suggests women who breastfeed lower their chances of breast cancer.

Possible disadvantages

POSSIBLE DISADVANTAGES or inconveniences may include: Mom is the only one who can feed the baby (but expressed milk can be bottlefed by others); sore, cracked or bleeding nipples (usually avoidable or goes away within two weeks with proper positioning); painful breast engorgement or infections (mastitis in mom or yeast infections in baby called "thrush"); breasts leaking at inappropriate times such as at work or during sex (leaking may eventually stop and nursing pads can be worn inside a bra until it does); there's no way to tell exactly how much milk baby consumes (but you can judge by checking numbers of wet diapers and weight gain); moms may feel drained and more tired (but even bottlefeeding moms are tired); restrictions on mother's diet, on drugs (including the birth control pill), on alcohol consumption and on clothing; possible discomfort by moms or others at nursing in public (but it's possible to schedule nursing around public "appearances"); ups and downs in the process, possibly for several weeks, where nursing will go well, then develop problems, then get better again (but bottlefeeding may also have ups and downs); possible need for breast pumping at work and preparing bottles for baby when mom returns to work.

Breastfeeding moms who have had good experiences say not to let the above list scare you (thus the parentheses containing qualifiers). Many of the disadvantages are minor and advantages usually far outweigh the disadvantages. For example, your dress and your diet may not be a big deal to alter (you probably were eating well during pregnancy anyway). And you may never have mastitis or bleeding nipples, or can prevent them. If you are educated, motivated, committed and supported about breastfeeding, you may be able to head off problems and breastfeeding may be a beautiful experience for you.

Basic breastfeeding information

- For the first days after birth, and sometimes before, colostrum, not milk, is produced, which is chock-full of antibodies, protein and other good stuff for newborns.
- When the milk "comes in," which may be from the second to seventh day after birth, breasts

may be hot, hard and painful (engorged). (The degree of discomfort varies from woman to woman, but if it's any consolation, it's usually less painful with a second baby and it usually lasts one or two days.)

To avoid or ease this, women can nurse frequently and massage their breasts from the armpit toward the nipple when you feel the changes taking place. Nursing, or using a breast pump or manually expressing milk, helps relieve the blockage, so nurse frequently. Contact your doctor or midwife for more suggestions or to ask about medication.

- Even if the baby is fussy, take a minute to make mom comfortable. Gather several pillows, grab a glass of water or juice, put feet on a stool and settle in a comfortable chair.
- How the baby is held has a lot to do with mom's comfort and the baby's success at nursing. Also, using different positions means different areas of the breast will be drained and different parts of the nipple used, cutting down on soreness.

    Most often mothers cradle their babies, turning them so the baby's and the mom's stomachs touch. Don't worry about seeing the baby's face or about the baby smothering; draw back the breast from the baby's nose, if necessary. Put the baby's lower arm towards your waist and cradle baby's head and back with your arm. You can do this lying down or sitting. If you're sitting, a pillow under the baby and/or your feet propped up may be more comfortable.

    For the "football hold," rest the baby on a pillow, holding under his/her back as if you were carrying a football, lifting the head to the breast.
- Newborns instinctively "root" for the nipple, turning their heads toward it. Help by brushing the baby's mouth or cheek with the nipple, and the baby will open its mouth. Push the breast back from the areola using thumb and fingers in

How the baby is held has a lot to do with mom's comfort and the baby's success at nursing

35

a semi-circle, not a pinch.

- When the baby "latches on," make sure as much of the areola is in the baby's mouth as possible. You may need to press on the chin to help open the mouth widely. The baby's jaws should be moving, rather than sucking cheeks in, and you may hear or see swallowing. Correct positioning helps avoid or ease sore nipples in many women.
- When the baby is done or you need to interrupt nursing, insert your finger in the corner of baby's mouth to break the suction. Otherwise, pulling a sucking baby off can be extremely painful.
- Babies may be finished when they fall asleep, turn away, let milk drain out or spit it out. Sometimes they fall asleep after getting just a bit of warm milk, and they need to be awakened to finish the feeding. Parents can wipe the baby's face with a wet washcloth or change a diaper to help the baby wake up. Generally, nursing time runs 10 minutes on each breast.
- Newborns will want to nurse every two or three hours. Wait too much longer than that and you may have engorged breasts.
- Babies usually get all the milk they need in less than 10 minutes, but they may want to nurse longer, even 20 minutes per breast. Let your baby nurse if it's comfortable and convenient for both of you, since nursing satisfies the sucking instinct. FYI, sucking is more aggressive on the first breast when the baby is hungry, so baby will empty the first one faster.
- Try to nurse at both breasts at each feeding. However, some newborns may only need one "breastful" at first, and some moms may be advised to empty one breast so baby will get both "foremilk" and "hindmilk." Ask your health professional or nursing advisor.

    Some mothers wear a safety pin on a bra strap over the breast where they finished at the last feeding, or change a ring from one hand to another, so they know to start there next time.

If one nipple is more sore than the other, start with the least sore breast first.

- After breastfeeding is well established, a bottle of expressed milk or formula can introduce the baby to a bottle. That may make for an easier transition when weaning or when mom returns to work and a bottle becomes a necessity. Some experts recommend waiting for three weeks or more to introduce a bottle, and then having someone other than mom offer it to the baby.
- Store breast milk for up to 24 hours (some say 48 hours) in a clean, plastic refrigerator container or bottle. Frozen breast milk can be kept for two weeks (in a plastic container or bag), though some women freeze it for up to a few months in a deep (chest-type) freezer (be sure to label containers with the date to keep track of freshness). Also, storing breast milk in glass containers is not recommended.
- Defrost frozen breastmilk by placing the plastic container in warm water or by thawing slowly in the refrigerator. Defrosting in a microwave or by placing in boiling water is not recommended because nutrients and antibodies may be lost at high temperatures.

Nipple care

NOT SO LONG AGO, gruesome-sounding methods of nipple toughening before giving birth were recommended. Now, no special nipple preparation is recommended unless inverted nipples are present. In that case, women can buy nipple shields to wear before giving birth. Other suggestions:

No special preparation is recommended unless inverted nipples are present

- Do not use soap, lotions or anything on nipples except water, since other substances may dry or clog nipples.
- Massage a little colostrum or breastmilk on your nipples after each feeding, then let them air dry or use a hair dryer for speed. Likewise, change breast pads when wet to keep nipples dry.

- Check to make sure the baby has the areola in its mouth, not just the nipple, and that holding positions are used correctly.
- The baby's tongue should be under the nipple, not up on the roof of the mouth.
- An ice cube on sore nipples may help before feeding. Some doctors prescribe lanolin for sore nipples (but not for those allergic to wool).

Diet and breastfeeding

WHAT GOES INTO a breastfeeding mom is passed on through breastmilk to baby. One mother who enjoyed fresh spring rhubarb pie claimed her baby's diapers smelled like rhubarb soon thereafter.

That means do not resume taking birth control pills, for instance, but check with your doctor to see what drugs are safe to take while nursing. (You can always "pump and dump" if you need to express milk while taking a medication for a few days.) Alcohol, a glass of which used to be recommended to help a new mom relax, now usually is not recommended while breastfeeding. Fresh water fish may need to be avoided because of high mercury or PCB levels.

Foods breastfeeding moms eat that may upset the baby's stomach include spicy foods, homemade herb teas, lots of fruit (rhubarb or prunes, especially) and gas-producing vegetables such as cauliflower, broccoli, beans, cabbage, sauerkraut, onion and garlic.

What you'll need to get started

- Breast pads, either washable cotton or disposable (cut-up diapers or sanitary pads work in a pinch) to use inside your bra for leaking.
- A nursing bra or two or three (many women don't buy this until after their milk comes in, as a pre-birth size may not fit; or buy just one that is one cup size bigger and one chest size around larger than what you wore in your last trimester).
- A few plastic bottles, eight-ounce size (though newborns won't drink more than four ounces, usually just one or two ounces in the first weeks), newborn-sized silicone or vinyl nipples

and covers—useful even if you are going to express milk and store it. (A bottle "starting kit" will cover this, or be prepared to choose from several styles and types in the store.) If you choose the "disposable bottle" type made by Playtex and others, you can store the refrigerated or frozen milk in the plastic "bottles" (really "bottle liners").

- A can of formula, powdered, liquid or concentrate, in case of emergencies.

Optional, or to be purchased later:

- Breast pump. Many nursing mothers wouldn't do without one because they can express milk and leave the babysitter with a bottle, or relieve engorgement fairly quickly. Others hand-express milk when necessary and never get the hang of a pump. Pumps can be electric, battery-operated or manual. Electric are most expensive (but don't need replaceable batteries), come in regular and travel sizes and are often preferred over the battery types. Often a hospital or clinic or nursing support group will rent pumps. Check with a health professional or lactation consultant before buying or renting a pump about specific types and brands.

Often a hospital or clinic or nursing support group will rent pumps

- Special nursing gowns or shirts that have openings near the breast, so moms don't need to lift up the clothing from the waist or below.

Many books have been written about breastfeeding, so this section is limited. You may want to consult the following books, available through the La Leche League International catalog (708-451-1891) or in bookstores or libraries:

Resources

A Mother's Guide to Milk Expression and Breast Pumps, by Nicole Bernshaw;

Bestfeeding: Getting Breastfeeding Right for You, by Mary Renfrew, Chloe Fisher and Suzanne Arms;

Nursing Your Baby, by Karen Pryor and Gale Pryor;

The Breastfeeding Answer Book by Nancy Mohrbacher and Julie Stock;

The Politics of Breastfeeding by Gabrielle Palmer;

The Womanly Art of Breastfeeding by La Leche League International (also on audio tape);

The Working Woman's Guide to Breastfeeding, by Nancy Dana and Anne Price, also authors of *Successful Breastfeeding*.

Bottlefeeding

If you bottlefeed out of choice or necessity, don't feel guilty. Millions of babies—and nearly all adopted ones—have been bottlefed. If the water mixed with formula is chlorinated, as most city water systems in this country are, and if the bottles are clean and other precautions are taken, there's no reason to worry about terrible diarrhea or other problems attributed to bottlefeeding in developing countries.

In addition, many mothers end up bottlefeeding within a few months (by age 6 months, 80 percent of breastfed babies in this country are weaned). While breast milk is viewed as ideal for baby, the bonding and warmth usually experienced nursing can be shared while bottlefeeding, as well.

The bonding and warmth usually experienced nursing can be shared while bottlefeeding as well.

Advantages of bottlefeeding

MOM ISN'T TIED DOWN and can get more sleep because anyone can feed the baby, anytime, anywhere; mom can return to work without expressing milk; once milk comes in and then dries up, physical discomfort associated with nursing go away quickly; mom has no dietary, drug, or clothing restrictions; parents know how much baby is eating; baby may eat less often, stay "full" longer, and sleep longer and that is less tiring than breastfeeding every two hours; resuming sex probably won't be affected by leaking breasts.

Possible disadvantages

POSSIBLE DISADVANTAGES or inconveniences may include: The biggest ones are health-related for both mom and baby. Bottlefeeding does not help the uterus return to normal, as does breastfeeding, and babies don't get disease- and allergy-resistance. Also,

40

formula may irritate some babies, requiring parents to experiment with different types; inconvenience of washing and preparing bottles; expense of buying formula and bottle supplies; some feel it's easier to overfeed an infant who is bottlefed, and overfed infants tend to spit up more.

- Make bottlefeeding a loving event. Cuddle the baby—don't prop up a bottle—and offer skin-to-skin contact when possible. When baby's done feeding, continue rocking, cooing and cuddling. Consider giving a bottle of water or a pacifier if baby's need to suck continues when the formula is consumed.
- Ask your pediatrician what formula to buy. An iron-fortified formula may be recommended.
- You may want to start off with one or two cans of powder or concentrate. In the long-run, you'll want to buy this stuff by the case to save money.
- Formula comes in powder (cheapest), concentrate (next cheapest) and full-strength/ready-to-use (most expensive).
- *Read the directions.* Diluting formula incorrectly can lead to serious nutritional problems. For the powder, use the scoop in the can; don't try to substitute measuring spoons.
- Powdered formula can be mixed ahead of time (make a day's worth of bottles and refrigerate.) An opened can of powder does not need to be refrigerated and can last for weeks.
- Sometimes undissolved powder clogs the nipple, so you may need to pinch it and stir or shake well before feeding (and sometimes during feedings).
- Shaking formula made from powder often produces a lot of bubbles, and baby may have more gas (or spit-up) and need to be burped more often. (To reduce gassiness, instead of shaking, stir formula with a whisk or spatula used exclusively for formula-making, and prepare formula the night before use so it can "settle." Also, skim

Basic bottlefeeding information

Read the directions

41

foam off top before pouring into bottles.)

- Concentrated formula also can be mixed with water right in the bottles or in bulk in a covered refrigerator bottle. Read directions for how to store unused concentrate and for how long; usually it can be covered and stored in the refrigerator for up to 48 hours.
- Ready-to-use formula comes in big cans or four and eight-ounces sizes, ready to pour into a bottle or, in some brands, ready to snap on a nipple. The small sizes are convenient for travel and, once the nipple is removed, are disposable.
- Always wash off the top of the formula can before opening it—and the can opener, too—or germs can contaminate the formula.
- Don't buy dented cans or those whose freshness dates have expired. Don't store formula in a hot place or let liquid formula get close to freezing. If liquid formula has separated or smells bad, return it to the store even if the freshness date has not expired.

Make small bottles of two or three ounces

- Four-ounces (half of a large, eight-ounce baby bottle) usually are enough for one feeding (many newborns drink only one or two ounces at a time). The safest bet is to throw away any formula not consumed at one feeding since "backwash" from baby's mouth puts bacteria into the remainder. Make small bottles of two or three ounces.

Types of bottles

BOTTLES COME in four or eight-ounce sizes, glass, plastic or disposable.

Glass bottles, of course, can break and are heavy, but it is easy to see if they are clean or clogged. Forget the decorative ones until you get the hang of this; you'll want to see inside quickly and clearly.

Forget the decorative ones until you get the hang of it

Plastic bottles won't break and are lighter than glass. Some clear plastic are as easy to see through as glass. Tinted plastic may prevent light from destroying some nutrients in the milk, and it is recommended for storing breastmilk.

The other option is "disposables," which is a bit misleading. The plastic "nursers" themselves are used over and over. They are bottomless and fitted with nipples and caps. They are filled with disposable liners, stretched over the top and then capped with nipples and rings.

The liners contain formula (or breast milk) and are thrown out, saving massive scrubbing of insides of bottles (but adding to household plastic waste). The other advantage is that the liners collapse as the formula is consumed, so less air is ingested. But the liners can be tricky and time-consuming and are hard to prepare with one hand (most likely, you are holding a crying baby with the other hand).

If you choose this type, don't forget to buy liners as well as bottles, and beware that this system is more expensive than glass or plastic bottles.

Some manufacturers offer a "starter kit." But still read the list below on what you'll need. And don't be afraid to mix products made by different manufacturers—for instance, one may only make rubber nipples for its bottles, but another makes silicone nipples that fit several manufacturer's bottles.

Heating a bottle

FIRST OF ALL, babies don't require that bottles be very warm; super-cold milk can produce tummy-aches in young babies, but cool should be acceptable, and room temperature is fine. A lot of parents prepare several bottles of formula at once and put them in the refrigerator, then heat briefly. A warm bottle seems more attractive to new parents and grandparents as it is most like the temperature of breast milk.

Babies don't require that bottles be very warm

Traditionally, parents ran a bottle under a hot faucet or put it in a pan of hot or boiling water on the stove, then shook it up and "tested" a few drops on their wrist.

Electric bottle warmers can be purchased. Parents insert the bottle and wait, then test the formula on the wrist.

With the advent of the microwave in so many homes, however, waiting that long with a hungry, screaming baby seems unnecessary.

Nearly everyone—health care people, books and publications, bottle manufacturers and formula companies—cautions against the use of a microwave to warm bottles.

Microwaves do not heat formula equally

Microwaves do not heat formula equally, so baby may get a burning mouthful of extremely hot liquid. Also, disposable bottle liners may burst. That might not be so bad in the microwave, which you simply clean up. But at least one baby has been tragically burned when the explosion occurred as baby started to nurse.

Nevertheless, lots of parents do it. Unfortunately, if this book gave directions for microwaving bottles, it might appear that the author is advocating that as a method of heating, which she is not. As one health care professional put it, "one tragic accident can scar a child for life. Better to let the baby cry for five minutes." It may help to remember the bottle doesn't need to be thoroughly warm, just not icy cold. Below are some time-savers for making warm bottles.

Time savers

IF YOU AND YOUR BABY don't sleep in the kitchen, and you are up several times during the night, these ideas may help speed up night-time (or anytime) feedings:

- Buy a special refrigerator container used only to mix and store formula, and mix up a batch of powder or liquid concentrate in advance.
- Get out the ice chest or cooler and pack it with some ice. Fill a bottle or two and place them in the cooler before bed. Parents can warm a bottle later under hot running water in the tub or bathroom sink.
- Mix concentrated liquid formula in a bottle with only a small part of the necessary water, or none at all. Refrigerate or pack bottles in an ice chest. Fill a "hot pot" or carafe with hot or sterilized hot water before bed. Use this water to mix the

Fill a "hot pot" or carafe with hot or sterilized hot water before bed remainder of the formula during the night (or, if your tap water is safe, use hot tap water). Shake well to make sure the temperature equalizes.

- If you use canned formula, buy a special can opener used *only* for opening cans of formula. Keep it clean. Put it back right after you use and wash it and you won't have to hunt around for an opener when you need one.

IT'S A GOOD IDEA to sterilize bottles, nipples and pacifiers before their first use. Get the water boiling, then put the items in and set a timer for five minutes. Pacifiers should boil for only two minutes. Any longer and the rubber in the nipples can break down. For bottles, place them on a rack in a kettle, if possible, remove them with tongs and drain on a clean rack. Boil the container you'll use to store the items, too.

In the "old days," parents would mix up a day's worth of formula, pour it into glass bottles, cap them and sterilize them by boiling for 25 minutes in a large pot. Then the bottles were cooled, refrigerated and reheated when needed. That happens rarely anymore.

If you live in an area where the water quality is questionable or you are using water from an untested well, sterilization, as above, is safest. Electric bottle sterilizers can be purchased. (Call your state or county health department to find out if they will test your water or who else will.)

Usually city water is chlorinated and thus need not be boiled before mixing with formula, nor do bottles need sterilizing before each use. Many people feel it's fine to run bottles and nipples through the dishwasher, then use either boiled water or hot or warm city tap water to mix the formula. Other parents without dishwashers don't sterilize bottles and nipples but wash them well with hot, soapy dishwater, using a bottle and nipple brush, and rinsing well in hot water, keeping them separate from other dishwashing.

Check with your pediatrician to see what's recommended for your area.

To sterilize or not to sterilize

Check with your pediatrician to see what's recommended for your area

Rubber nipples usually don't do well in the dishwasher. Vinyl or silicone, which last longer, are dishwasher safe. If in doubt, check the label on the package.

Also, remember that all your cleanliness efforts are for naught if you don't wash and rinse the top of the formula can or if you puncture it with a dirty can opener. You may wish to have a separate can opener that's used only for formula cans.

What you'll need to get started

You may want to change later because your baby simply doesn't like one type of nipple

DON'T BUY TOO many of any one type of bottles or nipples at first. The variety is tremendous; see for yourself at a well-stocked store (large national toy stores have a whole row of feeding supplies, as do large grocery, discount and baby stores). You may want to change later either because you find your baby simply doesn't like one type of nipple or because one bottle "system" is more convenient for you.

- Six to 10 bottles, most in the eight-ounce size. Your newborn usually won't need more than four ounces at a time, but the little bottles are outgrown in a few months, so don't buy many, if any, of these. (If you begin bottlefeeding in the hospital, you may receive sample four-ounce bottles that can be saved and used at home.) If you choose "disposable nursers," don't forget to buy the disposable liners.
- Nipples. The bottles you buy will have nipples. If they are rubber, also buy a couple silicone or vinyl nipples, called "orthodontic" (shaped for newborn's sucking needs) and in a special newborn size. You may want to try more than one kind or shape to see which your baby likes best.
- Caps or lids for the bottles. These may or may not come with the bottles. They keep bottles from leaking on outings and keep nipples clean. Buy one package at first.
- If you aren't using bottles with disposable liners, you'll need a bottle brush.
- Formula. Don't buy too much of one brand at first until you know your baby can tolerate it.

Optional, or can be purchased later:
- Electric bottlewarmers, for indoors or run by the car's cigarette heater (may take several minutes, which can seem like forever with a crying baby)
- Electric bottle sterilizers (usually not necessary)
- More, decorative or easy-to-hold bottles
- Nipples especially made for older babies or juice.

Burping

BABIES NEED to be burped after feeding to relieve gas, and both breastfed and bottlefed babies will appreciate the relief.

Some babies are gassier than others, and parents will catch on to how often or how much burping is needed. Generally, burp half-way through feedings or after every ounce or two, or if baby wants to stop unusually early in a feeding or is fussing while eating. The consequences of *not* burping may be crying or fussing after eating, inability to fall asleep, or spitting up.

Babies can be sat in your lap or held to your shoulder (with a cloth diaper or spit-up pad over your clothing—some milk may come out, too). If the baby is sitting in your lap, put your hand under the baby's chin; if baby is held up to your shoulder, put your hand at the back of the neck to support the newborn's head. Gently pat or rub his or her back until you hear the tell-tale burp. If those positions don't work, try lying the baby face down across your lap (again, with that spit-up pad in place), head up a little higher than body. Pat gently on the back.

YOU'VE SEEN, and perhaps been a bit repulsed by, those milky curds or stains on other mom's or dad's shoulders. Some babies—"spitters"—spit up after every

Spitting up

meal. Some rarely do. One theory is that the baby's digestive tract is still immature. Removing gas in a burp can also remove a little of the meal. Or baby doesn't know when to quit eating yet, and overfeeding can mean the "over" comes back out. Usually, if it hasn't been in there very long it won't be very curdy and isn't disgusting like adult vomit.

Keep a clean cloth diaper or lap pad with you during feeding and use it for burping (above). In fact, if you have a "spitter," just attach it permanently as if it were a new outgrowth to your shoulder, or a new parental clothing accessory, as there's no rule that spitting up is limited to immediately after feeding.

Spit-up may be reduced by reducing the amount of air baby is getting during feeding (use "disposable nurser" bottle systems and special newborn-sized nipples) and burping a few times during a feeding, rather than once at the end.

Stir, don't shake, powder concentrate formulas, or switch to liquid concentrate.

Clean the spit-up stains with a mix of baking soda and water, or use non-chlorine bleach directly on stains before washing.

If the baby is doing projectile vomiting, reminiscent of "the Exorcist," or if it's clearly vomit, call the pediatrician. Vomit *is* different than spit-up, and baby vomiting is more adult-like than you might think, and you'll probably know the difference right away.

Never give a young baby cow's milk. It has too much protein and some minerals, too little vitamins and iron, and is too hard on the baby's kidneys and digestive system. Babies should not be switched from breastmilk or formula to whole cow's milk until they are 12 months old or older.

Dipe 'n wipe

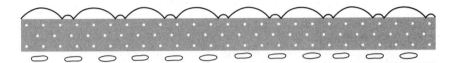

When to change a diaper may not seem like a question necessary to be asked by any thinking person. However, odor or leaking may be masked by super-absorbent diapers, and newborn's poop usually doesn't smell much.

Letting wet diapers go unchanged until fully saturated increases the chance of diaper rash and discomfort, not to mention leaks onto clothing and bedding. Letting dirty diapers go unchanged too long can mean a severely irritated bottom that may require a doctor's visit.

Put baby down and peek in the diaper leg openings sometimes. Diapers may need to be changed every time the baby eats (wait until afterward, unless your baby will not eat or cuddle until he or she is clean and dry), which can be every two hours, more or less, for newborns.

> **Diapers may need to be changed every time the baby eats**

Usually 10-12 diaper changes a day is the most a newborn will need (if the baby is wetting less than eight or so a day, call the pediatrician, as dehydration may be a serious concern). Anywhere from eight to 20 diaper changes per day may be normal for a newborn; with cloth diapers, which can't hide as much liquid, it'll be toward the more-frequent end of that range. (If you really can't figure out when a change is needed, there's a battery-powered diaper checker that meters diaper wetness from the outside of baby clothes; it retails for about $20.)

DIAPERS CAN, and will, need to be changed in many public places. At home, it's easiest to have a changing area at waist height where everything is within reach for the parent. If you are buying a changing table, buy one with a railing about five or six-inches high that goes all around the pad so baby can't roll off (they squiggle around more as they get older).

> **Where**

If you don't have a changing table, or are worried about baby flipping off it, use the floor, covered with a waterproof changing pad. *Don't* use the dining room or kitchen table unless you are prepared to disinfect it after every change.

Not every restroom has a diaper changing "station"

In public, not every restroom has a diaper changing "station." But they should. Find a large, level surface (or the floor) and cover it with your waterproof changing pad (which often comes with the diaper bag you bought). You can also buy waterproof pads, usually flannel-backed, separately. Or use clean diapers or receiving blankets in a pinch. You may wish to carry plastic bags into which dirty changing pads, diapers and diaper wraps can go until you get home. *[See section following on "What's in that diaper bag, anyway?"]*

How

GATHER EVERYTHING you need within arm's reach before undoing the dirty diaper. For the first month, you'll only need:

- a clean diaper, pins and (optional) cloth diaper cover and, if the diaper leaked, change of clothes,
- warm water and cotton balls (square or circular cotton pads may work better) or soft paper towels for washing,
- a small dry towel or washcloth for drying,
- something on which to lay the baby, such as a changing cloth or clean diaper.

Here goes

PLACE THE BABY face up on a changing table or clean surface, or on a diaper changing pad on the floor. Strap the baby in on the changing table or keep one hand on the baby at all times (though they can't yet turn over, their jerky motions can be enough to hoist themselves off whatever you've placed them on).

- With your free hand, remove the pins or tabs of the dirty diaper.
- Grasp the baby's feet in one hand and lift the baby's bottom off the dirty diaper.
- *If there's stool present,* use wet cotton balls or

pads to clean it off. If you're using disposables, drop the dirty pads onto the open diaper; with cloth diapers, drop the dirty pads on a tissue. Always wipe from the cleanest part—urethra/labia or penis/scrotum—to the dirtiest—rectum. After the baby is clean, fold the dirty diaper and remove it immediately, or baby's feet may kick into it.

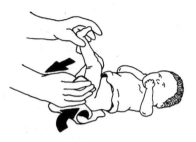

- *If the diaper is only wet,* you may want to fold the front part of the wet diaper under the baby's bottom (so the outside is under his/her bottom). Let go of the baby's feet and clean the baby with a wet cotton ball or pad.

- *Either way,* after cleaning, dry the baby off with cotton balls or pads or fragrance-free, white toilet tissue. Make sure to get in the skin folds between legs and torso. (You can air-dry if you want to take the risk of being wet or pooped on.)
- Lift baby by the feet again and slide the new, clean diaper under his or her bottom. Fasten the new diaper.

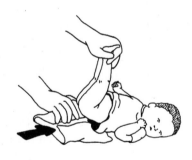

DIRTY DISPOSABLE DIAPERS should be folded so all fecal matter and urine is contained inside. Place them in a lined garbage pail (emptied frequently; it can go a day or two if you have a deodorant cake in the pail).

Home-laundered cloth diapers should be rinsed out in the toilet if there is a stool. While directions say to "shake off any stool into the toilet," you'll quickly find that newborn stool isn't shake-off-able (and probably won't be until he or she eats solids, at four months or later).

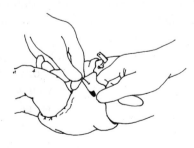

Instead, keep a pair of rubber gloves nearby just for this use, or buy a special pair of diaper tongs available in baby supply catalogs. Give the diaper a good dunking in the toilet, or even soak it there. Then hold onto the diaper and flush the toilet so the diaper is rinsed in the clear water filling up the tank. If the diaper is only wet, rinse it in either the toilet or sink, and wring it out.

Then place the diaper in a covered soaking pail *(see laundry section, p. 80)*. Make sure the diaper pail is tightly covered as children can drown in only a little water.

Most diaper services no longer require that their cloth diapers be rinsed. Instead, they provide a lined pail in which to place dirty diapers until pick-up.

Wash your hands! Baby poop doesn't come off just by rinsing - you need to use soap and scrub.

FOR GIRLS: Never wipe from the rectum forward, as it brings fecal bacteria into the urethra and vaginal area. Instead, wipe front-to-back (just as girls and women do after using the toilet to prevent bladder infections). Also, separate the labia and cleanse lightly to remove all matter. Do not scrub.

FOR BOYS: Zahn's Law of the Loaded Water Pistol: What gets a blast of cool air will go off. Plan to get squirted (and that he will wet his own clothes and maybe even squirt himself in the face) occasionally. (What the heck, plan for it every time, then be pleased when the loaded pistol doesn't go off.)

It's sterile when it
first comes out,
so laugh about it

When you get proficient at diapering, you'll be able to hold a wad of toilet tissue or a clean diaper over his penis while washing/drying with the other hand. It's only water, it's not very much, really, and it's sterile when it first comes out, so laugh about it!

Some parents prefer to point the penis down as they put on a new diaper. Otherwise, boys pee up and it may go out the top of the diaper, which often gaps at his waist (or what would be his waist, if he wasn't so chubby and actually could bend in the middle and sit up). Also, pointing the penis down until the umbilical cord falls off is one more step to ensure that the cord remains dry.

Make sure to clean under the scrotum, where fecal matter may hide. If your baby boy has not been circumcised, the foreskin does not yet retract. Don't try to make it do so—just wash it with the cotton pad.

If the newborn has just been circumcised, you probably received instruction in circumcision care. Some procedures involve a plastic ring that gets no special care, or a dab of petroleum jelly or antibiotic ointment. Other procedures involve a gauze pad that will need to be removed at each diaper change. Dab at the circumcision with a clean, wet cotton ball. You may have been instructed to apply petroleum jelly to the wound or to a new gauze pad, then rewrap the wound. (Look for discharge or odor and call the doctor if it appears to be infected.) *[See section on Circumcision section, page 70.]*

IF YOU HAVEN'T decided yet, or want to know more, see the "Diapering - Cloth or Disposables?" section in the Elimination chapter, following this one.

Using cloth diapers

Here are some hints:

- Traditional cloth diapers need pins (or diaper covers). Keep them stuck in a bar of soap and they'll slide through the cloth more easily.
- Put two fingers of your left hand (if you're right-handed) between the diaper and the baby so if the pin sticks someone, it's you.
- Beware of the possibility of pins unpinning and sticking your baby. Make sure you're not using a "kite" fold that has a pin in the middle over the genital area or stomach, which could be damaged by a loose pin. (This should not happen, however, if you are using diaper pins—not safety pins—that have a safety latch.)
- If the cloth diapers you bought or were given are not pre-folded, but rather the large rectangles, you have several options for how to fold them.

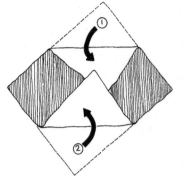

One way is illustrated here.

- If you can't get the knack of folding large diapers, use them for burp cloths.
- If the amount of cloth diaper between baby's legs is too bulky, give the diaper a half-turn before pinning. The bulk is reduced and there's a little extra absorbency in front.
- It's possible to "double diaper" a baby wearing cloth diapers to increase the absorbency.
- Make sure all of the cloth diaper remains inside the plastic pants or cover. Otherwise the part sticking out acts like a wick with moisture...

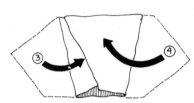

Other hints

- Disposable diapers usually have package directions and are decorated so you can tell the front (ones for boys have extra padding in the front; ones for girls have extra padding in the middle).
- Try not to get sticky tabs stuck to baby skin.
- For newborns, diapers (especially cloth) may have to be folded down in the front or back or both to make larger diapers fit.

- If the umbilical cord has not yet fallen off, fold the diaper down below it. For girls, fold the top of the diaper down and *out*. For boys, fold it down and *in* to prevent leaks (boys urinate up).

- Manufacturers note that solid stools should be shaken into the toilet, whether using disposable or cloth diapers. Note that for babies not yet eating solids, the stools are not formed and are too liquidy to "shake" off. Consider keeping a pair of rubber gloves near the toilet for this chore.

Since it's not a good idea, and sometimes illegal, to put untreated human waste into the garbage, particularly "full" disposables should be emptied into the toilet (but *never* flushed); cloth diapers can be soaked there (see above section on "What to do with the dirty ones").

- Diaper pails should be tightly covered (many come with a lock). Foot-pedal models are handy. Be careful of older children ingesting the deodorant cakes in some models.

- Changing pad, preferably waterproof, to put down on changing table, floor or other surface (such surfaces in public places are often dirty).
- Diapers—plan one every two hours and throw in an extra or two.
- Pins and clean waterproof pants or diaper covers, if using cloth diapers.
- Wet cotton balls or paper towels, in a sealed plastic bag—at least three or four per expected change, with one or two towels for *your* hands if there's nowhere else to wash up.
- A sealable plastic or washable bag for each of the dirty diapers and soiled clothes.
- If baby is bottlefed, a pre-mixed bottle, even if you just fed the baby. (Be paranoid. What if you have a flat tire and can't get home right away for the next feeding?) Pre-mixed formula can spoil if left unrefrigerated too long; you may want to put it in an insulated beverage container, then pour it into a clean bottle when needed.
- If baby is breastfed, an emergency packet of powdered formula, in case dad is out with baby and has the flat tire.
- As many clean outfits as you have clean diapers.
- Extra pacifiers.

Depending on how long you'll be gone, and where you're going, you may want:
- A bottle of formula, insulated in an ice pack or small cooler, kept in an insulated beverage

What's in that diaper bag, anyway?

Be paranoid. What if you have a flat tire and can't get home right away for the next feeding?

container until needed.
- An extra bottle for water.
- Extra blankets or pads for burping the baby on your (or a relative's) shoulders to catch spit-up.
- Extra shirt for parent when extra blanket or pad fails to catch it all.
- Extra layers of clothing, for weather changes.
- Extra nursing pads for nursing moms.
- Parent's needs—a snack, driver's license, sunglasses, handkerchiefs, car keys, make-up or hairbrush (not having to carry a purse is nice).

Elimination
"In one end, out the other"

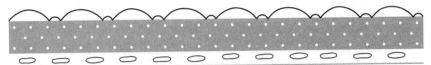

This is the chapter that's not particularly appealing, or often discussed in polite company. But it's terribly important to new parents who, perhaps because it's such a hush-hush topic, don't know what's "normal." Many new parents worry too much about the entire topic because their own baby will have its own "normal" standards.

Stools

WHEN IN THE WOMB, the baby's intestines contain meconium. It takes a few days after birth to pass all the meconium, which often is compared to black tar.

Then stools may become green or brown, and then they turn to yellow and pastey, often with "curds." (You know, it sounds disgusting, but it's not that bad when it's your own baby.)

It sounds disgusting, but it's not that bad when it's your own baby

But color, consistency and odor may vary. Usually a breastfed baby has several liquidy, golden-colored stools every day. The good news is that they don't smell particularly bad.

Formula-fed infants may have harder, darker and/or smellier stools that may be greenish from the iron content of the formula, but they, too, may change in color, consistency and odor.

Until babies eat solid food, neither type of stool is always horribly offensive (and stools from babies on soy-based formula may be less smelly than a dairy/lactose-based formula).

How often?

ONE BABY BOOK says, "A baby who wets 16 to 20 diapers a day is adequately fed." We should say so! And we should not wish 20 diaper changes on any new parent.

Babies urinate more often than they pass a stool, but, as newborns, it might seem like they're "going number 2" every time you turn around. At the most, babies may pass a soft stool every time they are fed, which might be every two hours, or so. On the other hand, frequency may vary widely over the first month (and beyond) and some babies may not have a bowel movement for a few days. Basically, the intestines, like the rest of the baby, have to figure out how to work now that the plumbing isn't connected to mom.

Is it diarrhea?

BABY STOOLS don't look like adult stools. After all, babies are on a liquid diet, so their stools are going to be liquid, too. Most newborns normally have what would be considered diarrhea in adults.

Real diarrhea is different and can be dangerous because it dehydrates the body. Diarrhea may involve mucus, be smelly and very watery, change color from what is normal, and will continue diaper after diaper, and maybe even during a diaper change.

The term "explosive diarrhea" is no joke. (More than one poor parent has been exploded upon at the changing table, as were the walls, curtains and table.) Even normal stools may make a gurgling sound or involve gas (harder stools may cause the baby to strain and get puffy-faced, but a baby may do that with soft stools, too).

Watery or explosive stools may mean sickness or irritation—but not necessarily. You'll soon get to know what is a normal variation for your own baby. If in doubt, call the pediatrician's office right away.

Constipation

"WHAT'S NORMAL is what's normal for you," one laxative company used to advertise. And that's true for babies. But even the stools of bottlefed babies, who ingest the same thing day after day, may vary.

Look to see if there's blood present, if the anus has cracked and bled, if pellets are present or if the stools are white—if so, call the doctor. Otherwise, hard or infrequent (up to a couple days) stools aren't usually a cause for alarm. Don't worry about occasional straining, and never administer a laxative.

Consult a pediatrician if you're really concerned. Many babies just use up nearly everything they're fed during a growth spurt so will eliminate less.

Like the "breast or bottle?" section, this is one the author may come to regret writing. It seems the subject generates a good deal of debate and passion. But, like breast or bottle, it's a choice new parents will have to make, and it's their business what they do.

Cloth or disposable diapers

It's amazing how many ways there are today to wrap a baby's bottom, so some information is necessary. Parents will have to choose between several types of disposables or cloth (cotton) diapers, either home-laundered or rented through a delivery service, if available. By the time this book is published, someone probably will have invented a new way to handle this age-old bodily function.

It's amazing how many ways there are today to wrap a baby's bottom

Even between cloth and disposables, there are now several types, options and "accessories." If you're undecided, perhaps it's best to go to a well-stocked baby or toy store (yes, toy stores carry diaper and other supplies) and examine the current options and prices.

Disposable diapers come in pre-determined sizes and have thicker linings in different places for boys and girls (buy "small" or "newborn," which aren't available in all brands). Most have elasticized waist and leg bands, which help prevent leaks. Some are thicker for overnight use; "ultra-absorbent" diapers probably have a gel packaged inside to hold more wetness than wood-pulp disposables—and they may hold much more liquid than a newborn can produce, especially when a newborn is changed every three or four hours, at the longest. At least one type of disposables, "Fitti," has pictures on the outside that turn color when the diaper is wet. Other types have areas cut out so the diaper won't irritate the healing belly button.

Cloth diapers now come in about four options: traditional fold-'em-and-pin-'em, traditional diapers with new diaper covers, new pre-formed cotton diapers with elastic waists and pinless closures—all of

59

which are home-laundered—or one of the first three types rented through a diaper service.

Traditional cloth diapers are usually made of cotton, and they come in gauze or birdseye weave. The gauze is more absorbent. They either come flat, like rectangular sheets, or pre-folded, which have a middle panel sewn in for extra absorbency. The squares or rectangles can be folded to fit babies at different size ranges. You can "double diaper"—use two—to increase absorbency. Cloth diapers can be used the way your parents did—pinned on at the side and covered with plastic or nylon pants, to trap leaks—or with new diaper covers.

The covers, which can be fairly expensive, fasten with VELCRO® tabs or snaps and can be waterproof, yet breathable. The clean cloth diaper is slipped inside the cover, so no pins are needed.

"Diaper Starter Kits" include diapers, accessories and a video to get new parents started.

There's another alternative to the traditional cloth diaper: a pre-folded version that has elasticized waists and legs and looks very much like a disposable. It may have snaps or VELCRO® closures, so pins aren't needed, and a waterproof outer cover. These are the most expensive home-laundered cloth alternative and may be available only by mail order in some areas (check advertisements in *Mothering* magazine).

Washable and disposable diaper "liners" also are available for cloth diapers.

A diaper service usually will pick up and drop off up to 100 diapers a week for newborns and provide a diaper pail and liners for storing the dirty ones. Some services prefer that you rinse dirty diapers out in the toilet; others let you shake off the you-know-what and just throw the dirty thing in the bag for pick-up later.

The debate rages on about which is "better."

Cost   A NEWBORN who goes through 10 diapers a day can rack up $2-$3 a day in disposable costs. Home laundering of re-usable cloth diapers is the cheapest method, however, it is not free, since they must be washed frequently in small loads of hot water. (Initial investment will be the cost of at least three dozen, which will be used up in two to three days). Plan to wash diapers every other day in loads of no more than three dozen (and preferably smaller, especially if you do not have a large-capacity washer).

MANY PARENTS and health care professionals believe disposables keep babies drier, because of absorbent gels and plastic linings, reducing the risk of diaper rash and general discomfort. On the other hand, the plastic lining prevents air from circulating. Disposables may contain perfumes or chemicals that irritate some babies. Cotton diapers "breathe," and the new diaper "covers" usually are "breathable." Because cloth diapers feel wet sooner than disposables, many parents change them more often than they would disposables, reducing the risk of diaper rash. Some babies' skin may be irritated by bleach required for sanitizing cloth diapers. Got all that?

Comfort

DISPOSABLES HAVE sticky tabs and don't need pins. Covers for cloth diapers use VELCRO® tabs tabs; covers or plastic pants are needed to prevent leaks; washable or disposable diaper liners are sold which increase absorbency. All of those options take a little more time.

Convenience

MANY DAY CARE CENTERS and day care homes cannot use or will not accept babies wearing cloth diapers. Bacteria in poopy diapers is more likely to stay put in disposables, which are less likely to leak, and which are thrown out, rather than soaked or recycled. Also, carelessly laundered cloth diapers can spread disease. (If you are careful, however, you need not worry about spreading disease by using cloth diapers at home.)

Germs

AT THIS WRITING, wide-scale composting and other recycling options for disposable diapers are being

Environment

61

researched. But in most areas, used disposables go straight from your garbage pail into the local landfill, where the plastic in them doesn't break down for dozens of years. Also, untreated human waste is added to the landfill. [Do not ever flush a disposable diaper.]

If you need to rationalize using disposables, you can say that virtually nothing in landfills decomposes because air does not circulate (and therefore aerobic bacteria cannot live and work) in buried garbage. Also, no more than 2 to 4 percent, depending on whose figures you use, of the solid waste in landfills is from disposed-of disposables. Unrecycled newspapers, or paper in general, takes up seven to 12 times more space in the dump, and may make up half the content of the landfill. On the other hand, Consumer Reports notes that one baby, before being toilet trained, could go through 6,000 disposables, compared to 50 cloth.

Parents may want to consider environmental concerns in their areas. Water issues may make cloth diapers unpopular in arid regions. Disposables may be frowned upon in places running short of landfill space (and taxes may be imposed through garbage haulers taking them away). Cloth diapers don't require trees to be chopped down to produce them.

Trial and error

FOR THE FIRST month or two, you may want to try one type of diaper and see how it works for you and your baby. You may find your baby's skin is irritated by one or the other.

Look at the bright side: your child may be wearing diapers for three years. You don't have to feel trapped into using one type that entire time. You may also want to alternate, using cloth during the day and more absorbent disposables at night, or using disposables infrequently during travel and outings.

Entertainment

"I get a kick out of vous"

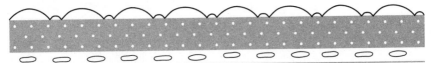

After those "heavy" chapters, it might be important to remember that babies are not all work and no play. OK, so they may be wide awake and ready to "play" at 3 a.m. But they'll get the hang of day vs. night soon. It's probably more important right now that you have some fun with your demanding-but-lovable new child. If you have never "played" with a very young baby before, or if you are just too tired at 3 a.m. to be very creative, this chapter is for you.

Thrills are cheap at this age, and parents should remember this when their little darling is 16 and wants the new car and $100 to spend the day at the amusement park with a gang of hoodlums whose very appearance would bring on cardiac arrest in their own parents.

For the first month, having a good meal and falling asleep on a warm parental stomach or chest is nirvana.

You need no fancy, expensive gadgets or toys for the first month. Manufacturers often put "birth to age such-and-such" on toy packages, but, in reality, that first month (or two) is not a big one for toys. A play gym, which has plastic dolls and mirrors hanging off a tripod, can engage a baby lying on his back, but probably not until toward the end of the first month, when eyesight and focusing improves. Black and white mobiles or pictures might be of interest to young babies (they can be purchased or made).

Those wind-up swings (by which many parents swear) *can* be used during baby's first month, but probably *should not* be used unless you have a very fussy baby on your hands *(see section on Crying, p. 20)*. Newborns need lots of neck and head support, so padding on both sides of the head with a rolled up

> For the first month, having a good meal and falling asleep on a warm parental stomach or chest is nirvana

towel or receiving blankets is necessary to keep baby from flopping around in the swing. Another negative of the swing is that it's not interactive with humans, meaning baby just vegetates there all alone, sort of like the infant equivalent of being placed in front of a TV set. For a 1-month-old, being held, cuddled and rocked is more beneficial to bonding and healthy development. (Later on, however, for parents of colicky or teething babies, those swings have meant they didn't have to spend Another Evening In Hell.)

Don't be depressed if your baby finds a 15 watt bulb more interesting than your face. It's nothing personal. And it will change. Soon he or she will prefer a ceiling fan over you.

Babies up to a month old like:
- finding their own hands and getting them in their own mouths
- finding anyone else's hand and getting a finger in their mouths
- rocking
- having an engaging face 10 inches away with interesting sounds coming out of it
- looking at black-and-white mobiles or designs
- looking at lamps or light bulbs
- listening to soothing music or "white noise," like fans or vacuum cleaners
- and looking at (and maybe grabbing, but not holding for long) baby toys like rattles or rings or plastic people or animals. A short attention span, that is, for stuff like the toys. Hours and hours, it might seem, for stuff like rocking.

Baby toys for newborns may be hard to find, since there aren't many. *See the "Shopping List" section for sources of where to find "toys" like black-and-white mobiles and designs.*

Let the games begin

IT'S TOO EARLY for many baby games, like peek-a-boo. But, if you've never played with a newborn, or you are terminally unimaginative, here are some suggestions for the waking hours (besides praying that baby will go back to sleep soon), with which you can improvise and ad lib:

"**Fred and Ginger**" - Nothing fancy here is necessary. Gentle swaying with babe in arms and you humming along to some big band music or old Neil Sedaka tunes, or whatever you can stomach. Be careful of baby's neck, especially on the dips.

Be careful of baby's neck, especially on the dips

Or you might sit on the floor, back against something, knees up and together. Place the baby's head at your knees with baby's body resting on your thighs. (Warning: If this gets really exciting, the baby may kick your stomach or chest, so this position may not be an option for engorged or nursing moms or those recovering from cesarean delivery.) Establish eye contact and play away (see below).

"**Jack and Meryl**" - Like Jack Nicholson and Meryl Streep in the movie, "Heartburn," sing all the songs you can think of with the word "baby" in them. (The '60s were "blessed" with baby songs, so start with the Supremes and Beatles. Since Sonny and Cher show no signs of reconciling at this writing, this may be the only good use for "I Got You, Babe.")

"**This Little Piggy Goes to Marquette**" - This is more for parent's amusement than baby's (at this stage, aren't they all?), but start with the big toe, and say, "This little piggy goes to Marquette." Then go down each toe. For each one, name a different scenic town in Michigan's Upper Peninsula or a private college known for its basketball team.

"**To Teacher, With Love**" - Raise one of baby's arms at a time and say, "Teacher, Teacher, call on me, please! I know the answer!" Switch arms and repeat. Good for encouraging interest in school.

"**Terminator-in-Training**" - Lift baby's arms and say, "Yes, I'm just like Arnold Schwarzenegger! Look at me—I'm so strong! Wheee!" Good for encouraging Hollywood to make violent movies that gross amazing amounts of money.

"**Travolta-in-Training**" - Swing baby's arms/

legs simultaneously to one side, then alternately up and down, and in the famous disco pose from "Saturday Night Fever," while singing BeeGees songs, "Disco Duck," or "The Theme From Shaft" (which, the author seems to recall, has very few words, most of which were "damn right" and "Shaft.")

"**Ahgoo, Ahgah, Ahgaré**"- Since baby's first word will probably be, "Ahgoo," or some variation thereof, might as well start now. You say it first, then give baby the opportunity. Other good words to throw in here are, "Goo-goo," "Boobly-boobly-boo," and a simple singing of the musical scale, "Do Re Mi."

(Zahn's Law of Baby Games: The more idiotic the adult looks, sounds or feels, the more baby enjoys it.)

Riding the Bike - Make the baby's legs go around like riding a bicycle in slow motion. Tell the baby, "Oh, he's/she's riding that bike," or anything else you want to say, since it doesn't make one iota of difference. Exercising the legs is good for them, though.

Loving Touch - Some practitioners of infant massage may start massaging babies at two weeks or so of age. Others caution against beginning before two months of age. You may wish to check with your baby's doctor or massage therapist, or both, if you want to start honest-to-goodness massages this early. Massage has been known to soothe restless babies, and all that touching from a loving parent is developmentally helpful. It can be a wonderful time for a parent and baby to just enjoy each other.

Even if it's not a complete body massage with oil at this age, babies enjoy having their arms, hands, legs and feet stroked gently. Stroke away from the torso down the limbs, and gently rub the belly, back, neck, head, feet and hands.

Classes in infant massage often are offered through certified and regulated schools of therapeutic massage, hospitals or groups offering infant care and development classes. Books and videos also are available.

For more help in how to play with your baby,

> The more idiotic the adult looks, sounds or feels, the more baby enjoys it

look for "You and Me," "Daddy and Me" or "Mommy and Me" classes through Early Childhood and Family Education programs, the YMCA or YWCA, or community education programs.

Skin care
"Soft as a baby's behind"

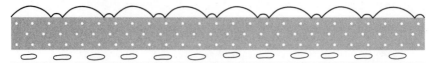

That doesn't even come close to describing the softness of a newborn's skin. It is so delicate, never having been exposed to anything but the ideal environment, that it is in danger of easy irritation.

Products

NEWBORN SKIN is perfect on its own, so forget about buying powders, oils, lotions, creams and other gunk to start. Those products may actually throw off thepH balance and *cause* rashes or irritation.

Powders can be dangerous if inhaled by a newborn

Powders—talcum, baby, whatever—actually can be dangerous if inhaled by a newborn. Don't use them on the baby and keep the baby away when you put them on you.

You will want to have on-hand several items within the first several weeks. All or none of these may be given you at the hospital:

- a mild baby-safe, unscented, non-drying soap or shampoo (one or the other; both are not necessary)
- special nail scissors with blunt ends (the clipper-things have been known to sheer off fingertips) for trimming nails while baby is sleeping,
- a bulb aspirator (a.k.a. a nasal syringe, "booger puller" or "snot sucker")
- petroleum jelly or other recommended ointment and bandages (for circumcision)

Also, buy:

- sterile cotton balls or cosmetic cotton squares (no swabs for ears and nose)
- and, perhaps, baby-sized wash cloths (much handier than large ones).

Avoid all products (shampoos, soaps, diaper wipes, for example) which contain dyes, fragrances or alcohol.

WHEN YOU LEAVE the hospital, the stump of the baby's umbilical cord is attached (and may be swollen). But it will dry up and fall off, leaving a "belly button." That takes usually less than two weeks (but don't worry if it's much longer).

While you are in the hospital, staff should demonstrate home cord care. Expect that four times a day, during diaper changes or a bath, you'll clean the cord with rubbing alcohol on a cotton swab or cotton ball.

Some health practitioners say to thoroughly moisten all of the cord. Others say swab only around the base, where the cord gets jelly-like. You may want to continue this practice three or four days after the dried cord has fallen off.

Don't worry about pain as there are no nerves in the cord. But if you have a newly circumcised baby boy, make sure no alcohol runs down from the cord onto his penis.

Do, however, use t-shirts, not one-piece shirts that snap over the diaper and cover and rub the cord. That helps keep shirts above the cord until it has fallen off.

Likewise, keep diapers below the cord. For girls, fold the top of the diaper out and down. For boys, who urinate up, fold the top of the diaper in and down. (You'll often have to fold over the tops of diapers for small newborns, anyway.) That should keep the cord from rubbing the diaper and becoming irritated or infected.

If it becomes very red or swollen, or if there is drainage or an offensive odor, call the doctor. Don't panic if there is a little blood when the dried cord stump falls off.

Some nurses and doctors say not to place the baby on its stomach to sleep until after the cord has fallen off. Instead, place the baby on its side, propped there by a rolled towel against its back and, if you like, one against its front, but well-away from its head. Some experts say just use one towel in back and lay the baby on its right side; others say the side doesn't matter; others say put a towel in front, too, well away from the face but keeping baby from flopping onto his or her tummy. (Most babies can't turn themselves completely over on purpose until they are about six months old). There's quite a debate about sleep position, however, so see that section.

Also, to keep the cord dry, newborns are limited to sponge baths until the cord has fallen off.

Circumcision care

IF THE NEWBORN boy has just been circumcised, you probably received instruction in his care. (An uncircumcised penis, for now, needs no care except external washing.) If you did not get instructions in circumcision care, call the pediatrician and ask details.

Depending on the procedure, there may be a gauze pad that will need to be removed at each diaper change. Dab at the circumcision with a clean, wet cotton ball. You may have been instructed to apply petroleum jelly to the wound or to a new gauze pad, then rewrap the wound.

Another procedure puts a plastic ring on the circumcised penis. No dressing is required. The ring usually falls off in a week or so. In either case, look for discharge or odor, indicating infection - call the doctor right away.

Bathing
"Slippery when wet"

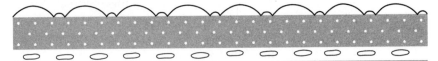

Bathing a newborn can be fun for parents and enjoyable for the baby, too. But lots of babies scream their heads off the first couple of times. If bathtime continues to be an ordeal, bathe only when absolutely necessary until baby's a little older.

A baby bath doesn't have to take hours or be very complicated, and there aren't a whole number of things parents can do wrong, except drop the baby. Perhaps the worst thing would be to leave the baby unattended on a table, sink, counter or whatever: "Slippery when wet" must have been invented by someone who bathed babies.

Sponge baths

NEWBORNS DON'T require the kind of vigorous cleaning that older children and adults do. Tub baths are not recommended until the umbilical cord has fallen off and healed, and the circumcision incision has healed.

Sponge baths two or three times a week are enough for one-month-olds. But wash face, hands and neck daily or a couple times a day, such as after feedings, with a washcloth. Wash the "diaper area" after every diaper change.

Bathing a baby right after s/he eats runs the risk of spitting up or defecating or both during the bath. A calm time, when the baby's not hungry or fussy, might be nicest.

Where

SPONGE BATHS can be given anywhere it's convenient—on a waterproof pad or towel in the crib, changing table, kitchen table, counter top. Usually it's most convenient to be near a water source.

It's important to be in a warm room without drafts. If it's winter and the heat has been turned down, consider warming the room where the bath will be given up to above 70 degrees. **Bathe only half the baby at a time**

71

the baby at a time, keeping the shirt or pants on while the other half is being washed and dried.

What   FOR A SPONGE BATH, get all of this together first:
- Two containers of warm water, one for washing, one for rinsing (test on your wrist or with your elbow)
- Two washcloths, preferably baby-sized, one for washing, one for rinsing
- Clean clothes
- Clean diaper
- Towel or waterproof pad under baby
- Towel or two to dry off
- Hooded receiving blanket
- Sterile cotton balls and swabs
- Rubbing alcohol for cleaning the umbilical cord
- Petroleum jelly (or prescribed ointment and gauze/bandage) for circumcision care
- Non-irritating, non-drying soap or shampoo (optional).

How
- Undress baby only half-way at a time for two reasons: babies cool off quickly, and some really don't like being undressed.
- Have all the products within reach. If you don't, carry the baby with you when going to get them.
- Talk to your baby while you bathe him or her!
- Pat all areas dry right after washing. Pay special attention to folds of skin.
- Lower your water heater to 130 or even 120 degrees. (Scalds account for 75 percent of burns in children under age 4.)
- Start at the head (supposedly the cleanest area, and work toward the dirtiest, you-know-where).
- Wet a cotton ball and wipe out one of baby's eyes, starting at the inside corner by the nose and ending outside. Discard the cotton ball and use a new one for the other eye (so as not to spread infection, if there is any).
- With the washcloth, moisten the hair and rub

the scalp. (If you are using shampoo or soap, squeeze *very little* on with your hand and massage.) Don't be afraid of the soft spot ("fontanel"), but be gentle.

- From the rinse water, use a wet washcloth to rinse. Immediately, gently pat to towel dry. Cover the baby's head with a hooded receiving blanket or dry towel to avoid heat loss.
- Rinse out the washcloth, sponge off the face, ears and neck, including all the folds. Pat dry and rinse out the washcloth.
- Remove the shirt. With the washcloth, wash the chest and tummy, under the arms, down the arms, the hands and the back. Pat dry. Rinse out the washcloth.
- Put on the clean shirt.
- Remove pants or leggings. With the washcloth, wash the feet and legs, again getting into all the folds. Pat dry and rinse out the washcloth.
- Clean the umbilical cord with rubbing alcohol on a cotton ball or swab, or as directed by your doctor.
- Remove the diaper (not one second sooner than you have to).
- With the washcloth, wash front to back (especially important with girls). Make sure to gently separate the labia (a vaginal discharge the first few days is normal; do not scrub vigorously) or wash the entire scrotum (do not pull back the foreskin of the penis). If the boy has been circumcised, wash the area and apply petroleum jelly or gauze bandage as directed. Pat dry.
- Put on a clean diaper (if you dare chance it, leave this off for awhile to facilitate air drying and reducing chances of diaper rash) and finish dressing the baby.

Tub bath

AFTER THE UMBILICAL cord (and circumcised penis) have healed, tub baths may be permitted (ask your doctor or nurse).

Bathing in the big bathroom tub, however, is difficult with a small baby. It's easier to be where mom or dad can bend over at waist height, rather than kneeling by the big tub. And it's easier at first if you have two adults to bathe one slippery baby. Or bathe baby in the tub with one parent, then have the other parent ready to take the baby when the bath is over.

It's easier at first if you have two adults to bathe one slippery baby

Consider buying a special baby tub (one with a slanted and padded back-rest is handy) or use a scrubbed and rinsed bathroom or kitchen sink pre-filled with two or three inches of water. For bathing in a sink, newborns might appreciate lying on a giant sponge, as long as baby is in a little water. (Then baby can recline without slipping, but parents *must* still hold on with one hand.) A large towel folded two or three times and put on the bottom of the clean sink will work.

A couple of notes:

- Soap or shampoo still aren't necessary (and make a newborn even slipperier) or should be used in very small amounts.
- Swing the nozzle of the kitchen faucet out of the way so the baby won't get bumped or dripped on.
- Never run water directly out of the faucet into the baby's tub or onto baby. Even if you have the temperature right, a sudden change (such as when someone else flushes the toilet or starts the dishwater) could be dangerous.
- Don't be disappointed if your baby cries as though this is some new torture to which to subject him or her. After all, baby has been warmly and securely bundled. Then the cold air hits warm skin and baby is no longer swaddled and secure. It may take several baths before it becomes less scary. Or simply wait. There's no

need to give tub baths, even for months—a sponge bath every couple days will do it.

- Fill tub first (and place sponge in the bottom, if you're using one); work quickly so water doesn't cool off too much.
- Eyes and face are cleaned as above (wash them before you put the baby into the tub to prevent eye contamination).
- Undress baby and calmly put baby down in the tub or on the sponge feet first, leaning baby back on your hand and arm, which support the neck. Wash with your free hand.
- To wash baby's back, lean baby forward onto the arm that just did the washing. Now wash the back with the arm that formerly supported baby's neck.
- Remove the clean baby to a dry towel and dry thoroughly (inside the folds of legs, neck, etc). Then diaper and clothe.

Other skin care concerns

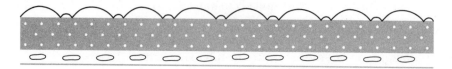

Newborns can suffer from a variety of skin conditions that may concern their parents.

Cradle cap

Massage the scalp with a washcloth and follow that with combing

NEWBORNS OFTEN go through a "molt," where new skin replaces the skin used in the wet womb environment. That also can result in a headful of dandruff.

Cradle cap, however, is noticeably different. It is yellow or orange scaly or crusty patches.

Even if the newborn has no hair, use a baby comb or toothbrush (used only for this purpose) every day to massage the scalp. During bathtime, massage the scalp with a washcloth and follow that with combing. In the winter or dry season, increase the humidity and perhaps massage a little baby oil or natural vegetable oil into the scalp.

If cradle cap appears, give oil massages with combing/brushing to remove the patches. A prescription cream or shampoo may be needed.

Newborn acne

NEWBORN ACNE is common and may be from the baby's raging hormones. It may appear as little pimples and whiteheads. Don't plug up the pores with creams or oils or use a drying soap. Just sponge-bathe the newborn, using a mild baby soap/shampoo or warm water alone. Acne and whiteheads go away (sometimes in a few weeks).

Prickly heat

Use loose fitting cotton clothing

PRICKLY HEAT can be a problem for summer newborns. It is a red rash found where the baby sweats, like leg and neck folds and where clothing binds. Use loose-fitting cotton clothing when possible. A little baking soda mixed in water and sponged onto the rash may help.

DIAPER RASH is believed to be caused by the irritation of wetness, rubbing and chafing of the diaper and in folds of skin, and skin contact with urine and stool. Once the skin's natural oils' protective barrier is broken down, the skin is susceptible to yeast in the stool. Prolonged, nasty cases of diaper rash can involve open sores that require yeast medication to cure.

Most newborns, however, don't get diaper rash right away. Peak time is 6 to 10 months of age.

The best preventative measure is a dry, clean diaper area—frequent diaper changes, washing with water and perhaps mild baby soap, but not baby wipes, then plenty of air. It's especially important to change poopy diapers as soon as possible. The problem in airing that area, of course, is that a newborn without a diaper is an accident waiting to happen.

Diaper rash can be cured or prevented by allowing a baby to nap on its stomach with its bottom exposed. Simply undo the diaper, leaving the diaper underneath the baby, or remove the whole thing and let baby pee on absorbent pads. (This will only work for a few weeks until baby can move around during sleep, so enjoy the immobility now.)

Allow the baby to nap on its stomach with its bottom exposed

Another preventative measure is to avoid plastic pants, which don't allow air to circulate. (Again, line the bassinet or crib with diapers or waterproof pads.)

Once diaper rash occurs in a newborn, phone the doctor's office before applying the ointment. Some doctors want to check to make sure it is diaper rash, and not a yeast infection, for instance, that requires different treatment.

If an over-the-counter ointment is selected, the American Academy of Pediatrics recommends "a bland ointment, such as one containing zinc oxide."

When baby is old enough for tub baths (after the cord has fallen off), adding baking soda to the bath water may help sooth the rash. Likewise, if you later use baby powder, pure cornstarch or a cornstarch-based powder may help, though some say it's not useful and may clog pores.

Jaundice

THIS ISN'T really a skin condition, but it shows up as yellow skin and yellow in the whites of the eyes. The yellowness may appear soon after returning home from the hospital, if not in the hospital. Estimates of the numbers of newborns with jaundice are as high as 80 percent. Essentially, the baby's liver isn't fully functioning and can't rid the bloodstream fast enough of old red blood cells. There are several types of jaundice, which the pediatrician can explain.

Call the pediatrician, but don't worry. Most cases of jaundice last only about a week and treatment may be as simple as altering feedings or exposing the baby to sunlight. Treatment does not necessarily mean the baby is very sick.

Sunburn and insect bites

Sunburn can happen very quickly, even in the winter

INSECT REPELLENTS and sunscreens can't be used at this age (some doctors recommend six months or older and then using special baby-formulated products). Sunburn can happen very quickly, even in the winter. So keep baby out of the sun and, in the summer, dress in cool cotton clothing. Insect bites can be prevented by placing mosquito netting over strollers or playpens.

Baby's laundry
"Rub a dub dub"

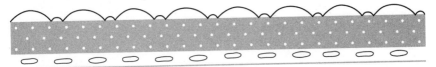

Laundry includes not only baby clothes, but receiving blankets, comforters, crib sheets, hats, bumper pads—virtually anything that touches baby skin. Even if it's brand new, wash it before use.

First of all, check the tags for the manufacturer's laundry recommendations. Then buy the appropriate detergent or soap and follow directions on the bottle or box.

Until babies are several months old (some say 2 years old), laundry should be washed in special baby soap or detergent, liquid or flakes. Other "adult" detergents may irritate your baby's sensitive skin.

Fabric softeners

SOME FABRIC softeners may irritate baby skin, too. What does not bother one baby may irritate the next.

In general, fabric softener "sheets" used in the dryer absorb less into material than the liquid ones put into the rinse cycle. But you may want to avoid their use altogether for the first month or more.

If you need to use a fabric softener for static reduction, add a liquid softener in the rinse cycle. Then run the load through an extra rinse cycle.

Do not use fabric softeners on cloth diapers because it coats them and ruins the absorbency.

Flame retardant fabrics

SOME FABRICS are flame retardant, especially recommended for sleepwear. Not all baby soap products preserve this, so check the labels on the soap boxes before buying.

Stains

PRE-TREATING or pre-soaking stains with baby laundry detergent and/or adult detergents or bleach may work fine as long as the garment is thoroughly washed in baby-safe detergent and thoroughly rinsed.

In general, you can rinse the garment, then apply

non-chlorine bleach or soak it in an enzyme stain remover before laundering as usual.

Run the load of laundry through an extra rinse cycle to avoid irritation

Be more concerned about the manufacturer's instructions, such as whether to use bleach, than whether it will irritate sensitive skin (run the load of laundry through an extra rinse cycle to avoid irritation).

For specific stain removal instructions, call the consumer services numbers listed on the detergent package or by the clothing manufacturer. The office may have a list it can send with stain removal directions.

Cloth diapers

CLOTH DIAPERS washed at home must be washed separately from all other laundry to keep from spreading bacteria.

Rinse the diaper in cold water immediately after changing (see Dipe 'n Wipe chapter, p.49).

Soak diapers waiting to be laundered in hot water with 1/2 cup of detergent or bleach per gallon of water.

Wash diapers separately

Wash only diapers—don't mix in other clothes. Use soap or detergent, plus chlorine bleach, in hot water, according to directions on the bottles or packages. Don't wash more than 36 diapers at once, preferably fewer. Rinse in cold water, then line or tumble dry.

Some parents say that chlorine bleach is too harsh for baby skin and that it is too harsh for diapers, making them wear out faster. They use Borateem, the 20-mule-team non-chlorine bleach.

Still, it's chlorine that really kills fecal germs (that's why they put it in swimming pools). If you use it, run the diapers through the rinse cycle twice.

Temperatures

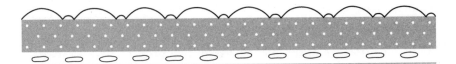

Babies don't need to be any warmer than adults, but newborns sometimes seem to have some trouble regulating their body temps. That usually is accomplished after the baby is a few days old.

Most parents tend to overdress, rather than underdress, their new babies. The best and easiest advice might be to just avoid drafts or setting bassinets in front of air conditioners, fans or drafty windows/doorways, and to "layer" clothing.

DON'T OVERDRESS summer newborns. Cotton clothes and caps can "breathe" better than synthetics. Put your fingers inside the neck of baby's shirt and feel for perspiration or coolness on the back and back of the neck. Check for perspiration in the folds of skin at the legs and neck (hands and feet aren't reliable indicators). Note that many babies don't develop the ability to perspire for a month or more, so don't judge completely by the absence of sweat.

Do keep your newborn out of the sun (even in the winter). Tender baby skin burns very quickly, and infants are too young for protective sunscreen lotions (sunscreen usually is not recommended for babies younger than six months). Also be careful of sun reflecting off of the water or sand.

For sleeping, figure the same amount and thickness of clothing you would wear, and add no more than one layer. For summer babies, a diaper, t-shirt and booties or socks under a light blanket or sheet is enough when it's hot.

When it's cooler, one-piece sleepers or pants with feet help hold in body heat, or add socks. A little cap helps retain body heat, too, at least until baby has a full head of hair for insulation. At this age, your

Keeping baby comfortable

Many babies don't develop the ability to perspire for a month or more

baby can't throw off a blanket if he or she is too hot, or add one if it's a cold night, so check carefully.

Taking your baby's temperature

THE ONLY RELIABLE way to tell a baby's temperature is to take it. However, don't take the baby's temperature regularly, just to know what it is. Don't take it if the baby doesn't feel really warm (or cold—a temperature *below* normal can indicate a possible infection, too) or if there are no other signs of illness, such as lethargy, or lack of appetite.

Buy a new digital thermometer (or you may get one in the hospital) that is made for both rectal and underarm use—it is easy to read and handle, works quickly and you don't have to worry about it breaking. Some models have pliable tips. Wash it according to directions on the package before using it for the first time (and certainly *after* each use).

The places to take a newborn's temperature are in the rectum or under the arm (a temperature can be taken in the ear but the special thermometer is expensive). Pediatricians often prefer a rectal temperature because they believe it to be closer to a true body temp. If the baby's been crying and upset, the body temperature will be higher than when baby is calm.

Normal temps

NORMAL *underarm* temperatures are 97.6 to 99.6 degrees Fahrenheit, though some say the range tops out at 98.6 degrees, like adults. Some doctors suggest not worrying until a newborn's underarm temperature is over 100 degrees.

Normal *rectal* temperature is slightly higher, 98 to 100.4 degrees Fahrenheit. If it is 101 or higher or 97 or lower, call the doctor.

(Under arm temps are usually one degree lower than actual body temp; rectal temps will read one degree higher than actual body temp.) This information is repeated below.

Underarm

NORMAL UNDERARM (also called axillary) temperatures are 97.6 to 99.6 degrees Fahrenheit, though some say

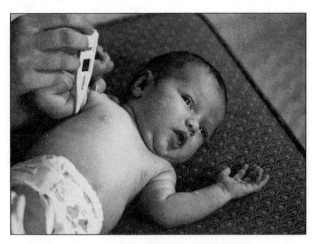

To take an underarm temperature, place the thermometer bulb in the baby's armpit and hold the arm down over it.

the range tops out at 98.6 degrees, like adults. Some doctors suggest not worrying until a newborn's underarm temperature is over 100 degrees.

Remove the baby's shirt and wipe the armpit dry. Hold the baby on your lap or a changing table, somewhere where a few minutes can pass comfortably.

Place the thermometer bulb in the baby's armpit and hold the arm down over it, to resemble a folded chicken wing. Wait at least three minutes to read the thermometer, preferably five, or until your brand of digital thermometer beeps.

THE NORMAL RECTAL temperature is slightly higher, 98 to 100.4 degrees Fahrenheit. If it is 101 or higher or 97 or lower, call the doctor.

Rectal

First of all, have diaper wipes, a lap cloth and a clean diaper ready because this may stimulate a bowel movement (use underarm method if the baby has been having diarrhea).

Lubricate the bulb end of the thermometer with petroleum jelly or lubricating gel.

One way is to place the baby on its stomach and remove the diaper. Another way is to place the baby

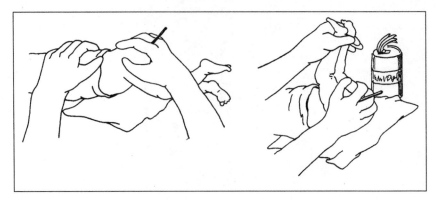

on its back and lift its feet, as during a diaper change.

Spread the buttocks and very slowly insert the thermometer into the rectum just past its silver bulb. When you feel resistance, stop and pull back a little. (Distance in should be about a half-inch. You may wish to measure the bulb and mark this distance on your thermometer with a permanent marking pen.)

Hold the thermometer with one hand flat on buttocks, with thermometer sticking between fingers, or hold the thermometer with one hand and the baby with the other. Time needed is usually one to two minutes, or until your brand of digital thermometer beeps.

After reading the thermometer, wipe it off with rubbing alcohol, and wash it before the next use.

If a fever is present or the temperature is below normal, call the pediatrician. Don't wait. Don't give the baby any medicine, but continue feedings or bottles of warm water. Dress the baby lightly and make sure the room is not hot.

Remember that fever is a symptom of infection or illness, not the problem in and of itself. (Depending on the illness, a child with a fever of 101 may be very sick while a child with a fever of 103 is not seriously ill. But this is for an older baby — do not wait to call the doctor for your newborn.)

Remember that fever is a symptom of infection or illness, not the problem in and of itself

SEVENTY TO 72 degrees is a recommended temperature range for newborns (they are happy at temperatures comfortable to most adults). Avoid fans, air conditioners or heat ducts that blow directly onto the baby, as new babies need a consistent temperature and are not good at cooling themselves off, then warming themselves up, and on and on. The hospital may outfit newborns in caps to avoid loss of body heat, even in air conditioning. (A noisy fan or air conditioner actually may help soothe a baby.)

Humidity is important during dry months, especially for sleeping. A room humidifier or vaporizer could be placed in the nursery. Make sure it's cleaned frequently (at least weekly, with diluted chlorine bleach) to avoid bacteria and mold growth, and don't let it blow directly into the bassinet or crib. Distilled water is best to use in ultrasonic humidifiers; some concern has been shown over mineral particles in undistilled water irritating baby's lungs. If you have a humidifier on your forced-air furnace, make sure the filters are replaced or cleaned before bringing baby home.

Safety first

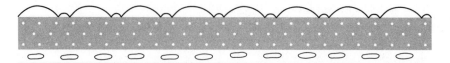

This book is not intended as a first aid or medical guide. It's a good idea to have those on-hand. But here are some basic safety precautions of which new parents should be aware:

Basic safety precautions

- Empty the crib, bassinet or playpen when baby sleeps to prevent suffocation. That means no pillows, stuffed animals or floppy toys. Don't lay babies face-down on super-soft pads, pillows or bean bag chairs into which they can sink. Don't cover the crib mattress in anything like a plastic garbage bag, dry cleaning bag or light plastic sheet. All of these things can block a newborn's breathing.
- For neck support, and because a newborn can't sit up, roll a towel or receiving blanket or buy a support pillow that goes around the newborn's head. You'll use this in the car seat, stroller and wind-up swing. (By the way, because newborns can't sit up, many umbrella strollers—the easy folding, simple-looking, portable one-seat strollers—don't give newborns the support they need, or are not sufficiently padded.)
- Make sure your stroller has seat belts and crotch straps and that you use them. Strollers should have a wide base to prevent tipping and brakes that work.
- Don't have aspirin around for children. It's been linked with Reye's Syndrome, which can be fatal. Never give a newborn anything the pediatrician hasn't recommended, anyway. When the baby is older, liquid acetaminophen can be used instead of aspirin.

- Don't use baby powder or talcum on a newborn because it can be inhaled into the baby's lungs.
- Never tie a pacifier (or any other items on a string) around a baby's neck. (This warning should be on all pacifier packages). Don't use homemade pacifiers. Pull on pacifiers and nipples frequently to make sure the nipple-part can't be sucked off and inhaled, and see that it has no holes or tears. The guard or shield around the nipple of the pacifier should be too big to fit in the baby's mouth and should have ventilation holes so the baby could breathe if it did get in there, anyhow.
- Keep toys on strings, drapery cords, laundry bags or other items with strings off the crib and away from newborns to avoid strangulation. Mobiles on cribs should be securely fastened and not have long strings or ribbons (remove them before the child can reach them).
- The slats of the crib should be no wider than 2-3/8-inches apart. Be sure to check, especially if using an antique, hand-me-down or second-hand crib. Mattresses should fit snugly up against the sides and there should be no corner posts. These precautions are to avoid suffocation.
- Crib or play gyms should be used only until the child is old enough to pull up and push up on hands and knees. Remove the gym when the baby is sleeping. (You may wish to use this only on the floor, with baby lying on a soft blanket.)
- If you have a playpen or portable crib with mesh sides, never use it with a side left down. Newborns could roll into the mesh pocket and suffocate. Better yet, don't use mesh-sided playpens.
- Never, not even once around the block, take your baby in the car without him or her being strapped in the car seat, and the car seat properly belted in the car (read manufacturer's directions). Car seat use is the law. And never use a carrier device or sling-type seat as a car seat.

The slats of the crib should be no wider than 2-3/8 inches apart

Never take your baby in the car without him or her being strapped in the car seat

- Changing tables should have safety straps and/ or railings to prevent the baby from falling off.
- Don't use honey in any food or on the pacifier for babies less than a year old. It can cause infant botulism.
- Don't put baby to bed with a bottle. Babies can choke or develop ear infections, tooth decay and other dental problems from having anything but water in their mouths overnight.
- Keep small toys away from small babies. Toys go automatically into mouths and choking can, and does, result. Newborns can't yet put toys in their mouths, but older siblings can. It's illegal for toy manufacturers to put small parts in toys for children under age three, but be especially careful of older toys with parts that can be pulled off, like teddy bear eyes, or parts that can break into small pieces. *Anything that fits into a toilet paper roll is too small for baby to have.*
- If you are using borrowed, hand-me-down or garage sale car seats, cribs or other equipment, check to make sure they are safe. Many times products are out-dated or have been recalled, but are passed along unknowingly to new parents.

  Guide to Baby Products, from Consumer Reports Books, by Sandra Jones with Werner Freitag, gives excellent information on everything from bassinets to walkers, including recalls and brand-name comparisons, plus clothing, baby food and diaper information.
- Install a smoke detector in the nursery.

Don't put baby to bed with a bottle

Choking

MANY NEW PARENTS are terrified their newborn is going to choke and they won't know what to do.

In reality, however, most choking occurs in older babies who can crawl or reach for small objects to put in their mouths. Choking, after all, comes from blockage of the windpipe with something like a grape, raisin, popcorn, peanuts, sliced carrots, a piece of hot dog, or a coin. Breastmilk or formula might accidentally get "down the wrong pipe," but usually is spit up.

That said, however, if the baby obviously is choking, can't breathe and/or is turning blue, call for emergency help at 911. (The medics can assist you over the phone.) Meanwhile, the American Academy of Pediatrics says to place the baby face and head down on your forearm, with your hand on baby's face and head, tipping baby down at about a 60-degree angle. Give four rapid back blows with the heel of your hand, striking high between the shoulder blades. (Silence when you should hear breathing means the windpipe is blocked—noise means air is passing through.)

If choking, artificial respiration, CPR and first aid are a concern to you, call the American Red Cross and inquire about taking a class in infant CPR and first aid.

Most choking occurs in older babies who can crawl or reach for small objects to put in their mouths

WHAT TO STOCK for that first month home? Don't worry about shopping 'til you drop here—you can get by with practically nothing.

The medicine chest

Almost everyone agrees that newborns should have little or nothing artificial put in them or on them. Their skin is nearly perfect the way it is and lotions and perfumed products run the risk of irritation. Therefore, keep the newborn out of the sun and away from mosquitoes, rather than using sunscreens or repellents.

Newborns should have little or nothing artificial put in them or on them

Many doctors do not recommend the use of baby wipes for diaper changes yet, but simply water and cotton balls or pads (square or circular pads may be easier to maneuver than balls).

Likewise, air is the best healer for diaper rash, not ointments, at this point. (Call the doctor if the baby gets diaper rash during the first month.)

Do not use baby powder which can be inhaled and damage newborn lungs. (Don't powder yourself around the baby, either.)

You will need rubbing alcohol, sterile cotton balls and swabs for cleaning the umbilical cord. Petroleum jelly or a prescribed ointment may be needed for circumcision care. A mild baby soap or shampoo usually can be used in small amounts without irritation for sponge baths. Nail scissors with blunt ends, a baby comb and brush, and a bulb aspirator for suctioning the nose and mouth are all desirable. Sometimes all of these are supplied in gift packs by the hospital.

When you do stock over-the-counter medicine, buy infant acetaminophen drops, not aspirin, which has been linked to Reye's Syndrome. At some point, you may want Syrup of Ipecac on hand to induce vomiting in case of accidental poisoning, but it should not be administered until the poison control agency has told you to do so (vomiting some poisons can be very damaging to the esophagus).

Car seats

OBTAINING this piece of baby equipment can't be put off because you'll need it for the car or taxi ride home from the hospital. Every state requires that infants ride in car seats, so one needs to be purchased or rented through a health insurance company or rental equipment company. Since many car seats fit infants only until they weigh 20 pounds (a hefty eater may reach that in three or four months), some parents choose to rent one.

Many models with various options exist. Basically, for infants, there are:

- bucket-shaped infant seats, with or without a carrying handle (they allegedly are portable), which fit newborns well and are good only to 20 pounds
- "convertibles" that can be converted to face forward for older babies and toddlers (often good until age 4), which stay in the car when you go indoors.

Spend a little time comparing

Spend a little time comparing. There are dozens of models; researching through *Consumers Reports* or getting the American Academy of Pediatrics' annual "shopping guide to car seats" are good ideas.

You may *not* want to use or buy a second-hand car seat because an older model may have been recalled (but see "additional resources," below).

Car seats should be easy to remove from the car so that baby can go into the grocery store without a 20-minute lifting-out-strapping-in production.

Car seats should
be easy to remove
from the car

Also, some parents use the car seat in the house as a sort of recliner-lounger for the newborn, so extra padding, a handle and washability might be considered (but don't get so much cushy padding that a baby could sink into it and suffocate).

In the car, the baby's seat faces the rear. If someone else is driving, ride in the back next to the baby in its car seat. If you are driving alone with the baby, the best bet is to continue to put the baby in the backseat. Do not turn around and fuss with the baby—pull over and stop the car, if necessary.

Make sure to read the manufacturer's instructions (and perhaps keep them in the car). Follow them and use both the seat belt and the harness properly. A special clip probably is necessary to secure the shoulder harness and lap belt combination. Some car owner's manuals have specific directions on the use of car seats in various models. The usefulness of the seat is undermined if you don't use it correctly.

Before buying a car seat, make sure it will "work" in your make of car. Some infant seats can't be used in particular styles of car seats (check instructions).

Often, back seats in cars slope down. That can mean the baby's seat will slope down, too, to the back of the vehicle seat. Baby's head may flop forward, and baby may have trouble breathing. Two rolled towels may help keep the baby's seat level. Put one under the baby's seat where it slopes down to the back of the vehicle seat. In addition to keeping baby's head from falling forward, the baby won't feel like he or she is riding standing up. Drape the other rolled towel from shoulder to shoulder around the top of baby's head. This supports the neck and keeps the head from rolling back and forth (this is the same as you'd do if using a wind-up swing). Cloth diapers, receiving blankets or other pads can be used for this. Make sure no padding is under the baby so that the car seat's straps don't fit too tightly.

Additional resources

- REQUEST NURSERY equipment safety information in writing from the Consumer Product Safety Commission, Washington DC 20207. Or look in the local phone book under U.S. Government to see if there is a local office. To hear taped information on recalls and safety information, or to make a product complaint, call toll-free 1-800-638-CPSC (2772). A teletypewriter to assist hearing-impaired callers is available, 1-800-638-8270. TTY for Maryland only, 1-800-492-8104. Or contact Eastern Regional Center, 6 World Trade Center, Vessey Street, Room 301, New York, NY 10048 (212-264-1125); Central Regional Center, 230 S. Dearborn St., Room 2945, Chicago, IL 60604 (312-353-8260), or Western Regional Center, 555 Battery Street, Room 401, San Francisco, CA 94111 (415-556-1816).
- For information on baby equipment safety standards, send a self-addressed, stamped envelope to the Juvenile Products Manufacturers Association, Safety Certification Seal Program, 2 H Greentree Centre, Suite 225, P.O. Box 955, Marlton, NJ 08053. (Look for its seal.)
- For a list of infant car seats, write for the "family shopping guide to car seats," American Academy of Pediatrics, Division of Public Education, P.O. Box 927, Elk Grove Village, IL 60007.
- Information on safe toys can be received by writing to Toy Booklets, Toy Manufacturers of America, P.O. Box 866, Madison Square Station, New York, NY 10159.
- *Guide to Baby Products,* from Consumer Reports Books, by Sandra Jones with Werner Freitag, gives information on equipment, including recalls and brand-name comparisons, plus clothing, baby food and diaper information.

Mom's physical health

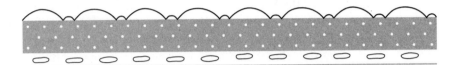

Now that nearly every conceivable topic on newborns has been covered, let's turn our attention to that superhuman who produced this beautiful baby and lived to tell about it. How and what might mom feel after coming home from the hospital and during that first month?

Involution/ "after pains"

CONTRACTIONS continue after delivery as the uterus works to return itself tr normal size and recover from delivery. Some women never feel them, other women ask for medication. Breastfeeding moms may notice cramping during nursing, since nursing stimulates production of oxytocin, which induces cramps. Both women who've had cesarean deliveries and those who delivered vaginally may feel these.

Cesarean delivery Moms

WHILE MOMS who had a cesarean delivery will stay in the hospital a little longer than moms who delivered vaginally, recovery at home may take even more time after what's considered major surgery.

Pain at the incision and general soreness in the abdomen, "after pains" of the uterus contracting back to its normal size, gas, constipation, pain when sitting, standing or walking are all among the possible after-effects. Expect to take sponge baths until the stitches or staples are removed (less than a week, often in the hospital) or dissolve.

One of the most difficult problems is not being able to lift and carry the new baby right away. But baby can be brought to mom and breastfeeding can be accomplished with baby lying on a pillow. (Pillows are good for laughing, coughing and sneezing, too.)

Cesarean delivery moms also may need extra emotional support. They probably were prepared for a vaginal birth. They may feel somehow they "failed" by having a cesarean. They may be frustrated by post-surgical limitations. They may just be disappointed that the "birthing experience" didn't live up to expectations. (So may Dads. Since a cesarean delivery is major surgery, IVs, surgical garb and anesthetics may mean that model birthing room scene, in which the baby is placed in mom's arms seconds after emerging, won't happen.)

Recovery may take several weeks, so try to arrange paternity leave or vacation time or a live-in helper for at least a week, preferably two or three weeks. Moms probably won't be able to lift and carry infants, climb stairs, drive or even take walks the way they would like to in the first two weeks.

Episiotomy care

MANY WOMEN dread having an episiotomy because recovery hurts. Stitches in the perineum dissolve and don't have to be removed. But that may take one to three weeks, during which time sitting, standing or coughing can be painful and the stitches may itch. Rubbing of a sanitary pad may produce more discomfort.

While in the hospital, instructions will be given on care of the episiotomy to avoid infection and promote healing. Care may include warm "sitz" baths a few times a day or squirting warm water over the area after urinating. Sometimes care includes the "cold" route with ice compresses. Medications may be prescribed, or try witch hazel applied with a cotton ball.

As with hemorrhoids, avoid sitting in one position for a long time, which strains the perineum. Indeed, the entire perineum, whether or not there's an episiotomy, may be sore after a vaginal birth.

Hemorrhoids

IF THE PRESSURE of the baby on the rectum during pregnancy didn't produce swollen varicose veins around the anus or inside the rectum (hemorrhoids), the strain of pushing during delivery might have. You'll recognize them by itching, burning, bleeding, pain or a feeling of pressure while having a bowel movement.

Treatment to reduce the swelling is the same as for episiotomy care—keep the area clean with sitz baths and don't sit in one position for a long time. Over-the-counter medications usually are recommended to reduce the itch and pain, or try witch hazel. Avoid constipation—straining results in more swelling—and eat high-fiber foods or take stool softeners, if necessary. Drink plenty of fluids, too. Keep the area clean. Recline as often as possible—feed and cuddle the baby lying down.

Lochia

THIS IS ESSENTIALLY dead uterine tissue being sloughed off. The discharge may continue for up to seven weeks. The discharge of blood and mucus should not contain large blood clots, and it should not be bright-red blood for more than several days. Tampons can't be used because of possible infection, so use sanitary pads. The color, amount and odor of the discharge may change over the weeks, but women who breastfeed may have lochia for a shorter "period." If you exercise heavier-than-usual, flow may increase. Call the doctor's office if there is pain or unusual cramping, or if more than one sanitary napkin is needed in an hour for a couple hours in a row, if the heavy flow also has a large number of blood clots, if the odor is bad, or if the discharge causes itching. In general, the flow shouldn't be heavier than on the heaviest day of your period. A fever greater than 100.4 degrees Fahrenheit or tenderness should also be reported to the doctor as a possible uterine infection.

Sleeplessness

LACK OF DEEP SLEEP is a bonafide form of torture. Funny thing, it's also a rite of parenthood.

Sleep when baby sleeps

Sleep when baby sleeps. (Everyone advises that, but you should really do it.) Let housework go, hire help or cut deals with friends or neighbors. Feed the baby right before you go to bed, which might mean the baby will sleep a little longer.

Some parents have split up for a night. One heads for the downstairs couch or sleeper sofa, a tent or

Do whatever
works for you and
don't worry about
what the neigh-
bors or relatives
will say

trailer in the backyard, or a motel. At least one of them can get a full-night's sleep.

Do whatever works for you and don't worry about what the neighbors or relatives will say. Lack of sleep colors how you feel about nearly everything else, including parenting.

Sore breasts

AT BIRTH, colostrum is present in the mother's breasts, but babies consume very little. On the second to seventh day after birth, breast milk "comes in." Breasts can be huge, painful, hot and hard. No new mother finds this fun. In fact, it's sort of one last rude little shock the body has for a woman whose body has already undergone dramatic change.

It may seem easiest to have a "hands off" response. But if you are breastfeeding, baby should be encouraged to nurse, breasts massaged and milk expressed to relieve the extra milk. (Expressing milk may be easier if it's done during a hot shower.) Nursing may be difficult because the nipples seem to be stretched out and hard for the baby to find and hold. If that's the case, try to express enough milk to relieve the swelling before starting to nurse.

If you are
breastfeeding,
baby should be
encouraged
to nurse

Sometimes engorgement can be lessened if the massage is started before the milk comes in. Hot compresses or pain medication may be recommended. Severe engorgement, blessedly, may last only a day.

Milk "comes in" for both breast- and bottle-feeding mothers. For those who are bottlefeeding, a few doctors will prescribe hormones in some cases to prevent engorgement. Even without a shot, the unused milk supply dries up in a few days or a week. Massage—even vigorous washing in the shower—encourages milk production and should be avoided or the milk production will continue. A supportive bra also might help make mom more comfortable.

Breasts may leak colostrum before birth and after, as well as milk. Nursing pads, cut-up or disposable diapers with plastic backing removed, sanitary pads, or cotton handkerchiefs can be worn inside a bra so moisture doesn't soak through. Change the pads often, however, to keep nipples dry.

Don't be surprised if your post-pregnancy breasts and nipples are not the same size or shape as your pre-pregnancy breasts. Give them a couple months before mourning or rejoicing over possibly-new breasts. Nipples may remain darker and breasts may have stretch marks.

PREGNANT MOTHERS who took a breather from the hormone roller coaster during pregnancy may find themselves back on the wild ride after birth. Weepiness for up to six weeks is common, and the "baby blues" may include anxiety and wide mood swings. Severe depression also may be a result of hormonal changes. So is excessive sweating and urination (the body is ridding itself of extra fluids). Hair loss is not unheard of. Especially in breastfeeding mothers, vaginal dryness can be a problem, and changing hormones may mean a loss of sex drive (or could it simply be exhaustion?). Contact your health care provider for more information and help, especially if depression is severe. Unfortunately, little is done for general weepiness, but don't hesitate to tell a doctor about depression. *[See "When You're All Alone Or Feel That Way" chapter, p. 101]*

Hormones

Weepiness for up to six weeks is common

USE CAUTION here and follow the professional advice given if taking up exercise in the first month is appealing. Remember the body has been taxed and modified, and joints and ligaments aren't yet up to doing what they did before pregnancy. Returning to pre-pregnancy weight or proportions is not worth injuring oneself. Heavy exercise also may increase the flow of lochia.

Still, safe exercise, such as walking, may speed recovery. Consult your doctor about when to begin an exercise regime and to recommend specific post-partum exercises that won't injure specific tissues or muscles. Remember to start slowly and to stop

Exercise

immediately if there is pain. Women who had a cesarean birth will have to wait patiently—even driving a car may not be recommended for two weeks.

New mothers may lose 10-15 pounds in the hospital

On the average, new mothers may lose 10-15 pounds in the hospital (weight of the baby plus up to 2 pounds each of placenta, amniotic fluid, and water/blood), and another three pounds or so in the next week as fluid retention is lost.

Nursing mothers need to continue a recommended calorie intake and vitamin and mineral supplements. Non-nursing moms should be careful to get enough vitamin and minerals, especially iron and calcium, to help their bodies recover.

Bowel and bladder

AFTER HAVING a vaginal delivery, constipation and inability to urinate is common in the hospital and may be strange for a few days at home. Drinking a lot of water and eating high-fiber foods usually take care of it. (Note that the amount of breast milk produced often is directly proportional to the amount of fluids consumed.)

During a cesarean delivery, the intestines are "shut down" by anesthesia and then have to restart. Also, surgery has allowed air into the abdominal cavity. Moms should expect abdominal gas and bloating, which can be extremely painful. A clear liquid diet, over-the-counter gas medications and walks should help. In addition, a catheter may have left the urethra sore, so don't soap up that area during a shower. Ask in the hospital about what to expect at home.

Finding a pediatrician
"The doctor is in"

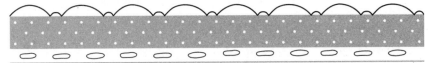

There's nothing more stressful for new parents than a sick baby. And when the baby's not sick, but you've got a question, a pediatrician's office often can be an excellent resource and source of support for new parents. Therefore, try to interview or seek a pediatric practice as soon as possible (or find a "family practice" doctor's office).

The pediatrician who examines (and perhaps circumcises) your baby in the hospital may be one you want to keep seeing. But many health insurance plans allow flexibility in choosing a pediatrician, and perhaps you wish to find another. How do you find and then choose a pediatrician?

How do you choose a pediatrician?

Pediatricians have three years of training in pediatric medicine after completing medical school. During the first year, you'll probably see a pediatrician for check-ups and possibly immunizations at age two weeks, and at two, four, six and nine months.

Note that some offices have pediatric nurse practitioners, similar to certified midwife nurse practitioners, who are not doctors but have special advanced training. They often handle routine matters and provide preventative health care for well babies, as well as answer questions. Their services often are less expensive than a pediatrician, and their appointment schedules may be more open.

The American Academy of Pediatrics will send parents a list of member pediatricians in their area. Write Department of Communications, American Academy of Pediatrics, P.O. Box 927, Elk Grove Village, IL 60009. The Academy has more than 41,000 members worldwide and its members must "demonstrate competence by passing a comprehensive certification examination, and they must provide evidence of high ethical standards and professionalism."

What to consider about a pediatric practice

WHEN TRYING to find a pediatrician, don't discard word-of-mouth as a good indicator. Friends or neighbors may have a trusting relationship with their child's doctor.

Make sure, however, that the reason that doctor is well-liked is because of traits important to *you*. For example, if you feel intimidated by an arrogant type when you ask innocent questions, you'd best find a doctor who is more down-to-earth. If you expect information to be offered without asking a lot of questions, find a take-charge doctor or clinic. If your family has a history of certain conditions, such as allergies, look for a doctor who specializes in that area.

Zahn's Law of Illness: Babies only get sick between the hours of 5 p.m. and 8 a.m., or on weekends. Off-hours availability, or at least a phone nurse reachable after office hours, is very important.

How easy is it to call and get an appointment made or a question answered?

Ask who will see your baby if your primary doctor is unavailable, and with what hospital or emergency clinic the pediatrician's practice is affiliated. How easy is it to call and get an appointment made or a question answered?

Don't overlook "crib-side manner." An adult may not care if a doctor is serious or has quick movements. A baby or toddler, though, given a choice, might prefer Mr. Rogers. Short of that, he or she may have to settle for someone who "is good with kids."

The American Academy of Pediatrics suggests the following:

"Ask the pediatrician about their medical background...In addition, ask the pediatrician about their practice and philosophy of care—do you agree on important issues such as preventive medicine, medical treatment, etc.?

"Inquire about the age range of the pediatrician's patients and any special arrangements—such as separate waiting rooms or office hours—for different age groups.

"When stopping by the pediatrician's office before your first appointment, look at the office. Is it child-oriented? Does the office staff greet the patients by name? Do you feel comfortable with the pediatrician and the office staff?

"How are your questions answered? The responses should be respectful and reassuring, not patronizing. In addition, does the pediatrician listen to your questions and give you an answer that relates to your question?

The responses should be respectful and reassuring, not patronizing

"Check office hours. Find out who is on duty during off hours and weekends and how emergencies are handled.

"Does the pediatrician perform routine exams?

"Review your health insurance policy to check which services will be covered—regular checkups, sick visits and immunizations. Check on the pediatrician's hospital affiliation.

"If the pediatrician is in a group practice, does anyone in the group have a subspecialty such as neurology, allergy, dermatology, etc.? Ask to meet the other doctors in the office since your child may have to see them if your pediatrician is not available."

THE BABY'S one or two-week check up includes a physical exam. Some doctors are beginning to give hepatitis immunizations at the two-week check-up, but usually shots are put off for another six weeks. (As parents, you decide when or if your child gets immunizations, and you may wish to read up on this subject and its ramifications.)

The first check-up

This is an opportunity to make sure the baby is gaining enough weight, to check for reflexes and proper development, and to answer parents' questions. (It sounds silly, but make a list before you go or you'll forget something).

Pets

"Welcome to the family, Baby . . . maybe"

The former "top dog" or "top cat" naturally may be jealous when you bring in the baby—right from the first step in the door. Dogs and cats are territorial animals. Make sure they are given as much extra attention as possible the first weeks home, as they are naturally threatened by the introduction of a younger, more demanding "sibling."

Introducing the baby

SOME EXPERTS suggest having dad bring home from the hospital a baby blanket or clothing item containing the baby's scent and letting the dog or cat sniff it *before* baby comes home.

Also, some experts suggest that mom (whose attention probably will be most missed as she probably spends the most time doing baby care) enter the house first, without the baby, and greet the dog. Then let dad (usually the "alpha male" pack leader in the dog's house) carry the baby in and lean down to let the dog sniff the new arrival (of course, mom will have to restrain a wildly leaping or overly friendly dog, and *especially* restrain an aggressive dog). It's important to have lots of immediate praise for a good dog who gently sniffs. If the dog does well, continue with *supervised* times of putting the baby on the floor where the dog can really sniff him or her thoroughly.

Have lots of immediate praise for a good dog who gently sniffs

For cats, some experts suggest feeding the cat when the baby arrives. The theory is that the cat will associate positive vibes with the baby. Also, let the cat sniff the baby when baby is relaxed or asleep, not screaming or fussing. A relaxed baby may calm the cat.

Never leave a pet alone with the newborn

For a couple months, at least, don't give the dog or cat free access to the baby's quarters, and *never* leave a pet alone with the newborn (though many dogs become protective and eventually may want to sleep in

102

the baby's room). The point is, this is new territory for the pet, and their reaction may be unpredictable.

It may be a nasty myth, some cat lover's say, about cats snuggling up with—and suffocating—sleeping babies who are too young to roll over and throw the cat off them. Better to be safe than sorry: keep a tight net or screen over the bassinet or crib so the cat can't climb in, should kitty obtain access to the nursery, or wherever baby is placed.

Neutering a cat several weeks before baby comes home may minimize aggressive behavior and may avoid the cat spraying the baby's belongings.

PETS WHICH have never been around babies or children, ideally, should be exposed to them under controlled conditions before the baby is born. If you have willing friends with new (or older) babies, ask if you can bring Fido along on a brief visit, or let Kitty play with the baby on a visit to your house. If there are neighborhood kids, see if you can introduce them. If you have the option of boarding your pet with an in-house service that places your pet with with a family, ask for a family with kids. Some new parents prefer to muzzle Fido while this contact or new-baby exposure is going on, just to be safe.

Minimizing risks

Dog owners, especially, should get in the habit of involving the dog in play or giving the dog attention while the baby is in the room and awake. At the same time, ignore the dog when baby is asleep. The purpose is to help the dog associate good times with an awake baby, rather than "I just get attention when that baby is asleep, so I want it to be asleep permanently."

If, after all, you suspect Fido or Kitty will not take kindly—ever—to your baby (perhaps it has bitten or scratched other children?), plan to house your pet completely separately, or, sad to say, consider finding a good home or euthanizing your companion. The fact of the matter is, you can't risk serious injury to your baby. Period.

If your pet has not been obedience trained, the

time to start is before the baby is born. Many an untrained dog has ended up banished to the end of a rope in the backyard—or sent to the pet shelter or put to sleep—because it would knock the baby over or cause other injuries, not out of malice, but because the owners never cared enough to train their pet.

If you are considering getting a new pet, wait

If you are considering getting a new pet, wait. Puppies and kittens are babies in their own right and have many baby-like demands, which deserve to be met. You do not need to be caring for two babies, human and canine or feline, at once.

Some experts believe the best time of a dog or cat's life to introduce babies to them is when the pet is 1-1/2 years to 4-years-old. They are settled down and through their own babyhood, but not so old to be too set in their ways.

Remember that pets are individuals, and you can't predict their reactions in all circumstances. If your pet has difficulty adjusting, you may want to consult with its veterinarian or a pet behavior specialist.

Allergies

Don't let the dog lick the newborn

BABIES MAY BE allergic to pet dander and/or pet saliva. Reactions may range from a rash where the dog licked to stopping breathing (call 911!). Watch the baby carefully when you bring him or her home. Don't let the dog lick the newborn. Tell the pediatrician before you leave the hospital that you have a pet at home and ask what to look for in terms of allergic reactions.

Cats actually can have physical reactions to newborns—some high-strung cats may develop skin or urination problems, and may need tranquilizers, steroids or other treatment.

Pet health and insecticides

ASK YOUR veterinarian, preferably during pregnancy, whether your pet should have any tests for parasites. Don't bring a new baby home to a house that has been freshly flea "bombed." Also, don't have the cat or dog wearing flea and tick collars, and don't douse your pets with flea killers with a new baby in the house. Talk with your veterinarian about these concerns.

Time

"And baby makes three"

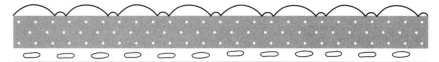

There are bound to be emotional, as well as physical, adjustments to parenthood (See *"Crying - Mom"* and *"Crying-Dad"* sections, too). And while Dad may not feel different physically, he may need some "recovery" time as well to adjust to his new role.

New parents typically report concerns about the increased sense of responsibility being a parent brings. Some parents feel trapped in a job or career because of heightened financial needs. Some feel guilty for taking unpaid time off work, or feel they can't afford to do so.

BUT ALL NEW parents experience a time crunch. There's no morning (or afternoon, or evening...) shower when someone is crying to be fed and held and changed. When Sunday mornings may have been spent reading the newspaper together, now, perhaps, one parent is up at the crack of dawn for a feeding/diapering/rocking routine, while the other toasts bread and washes dishes and does other glamorous chores while wearing pajamas that are a week "older" than the baby.

The time crunch

It's hard to pinpoint where the time goes, but it does. It's next to impossible to do anything but feed a baby, for instance, when you're feeding a baby (and it's designed that way; feeding is an important time for interaction). When you're not feeding a baby, what are you doing?

What did you get done while baby napped? You are lucky, some days, if you have time to brush your teeth. Sometimes women with a new baby are prone to bladder infections because they don't go to the bathroom often enough (through no fault of their own).

You are lucky, some days, if you have time to brush your teeth

- Remember, this is temporary.
- Cancel that newspaper subscription temporarily.

Hints

- Cultivate skills using one hand and/or deep knee bends. To start: Watering houseplants. Moving dirty dishes from one counter to the sink and back. Picking up mail and putting it in the garbage. Work up to holding the baby while you use the toilet.

Assume you will get nothing done except baby care

- Have no expectations. Assume you will get nothing done except baby care. *Nothing.* Then you will think it is a big deal if you can open the drapes.
- Have no expectations. Assume you will get nothing done except baby care. *Nothing.* Then you will think it is a big deal if you can open the drapes. (This hint has been brought to you again on purpose in case you weren't paying attention the first time. It's important!)

Other changes

YOU MAY BE noticing other changes. The way in which you "experience" parenthood may be joyous, resentful, apprehensive, cautious, angry, or all of the above, at different times. Your spouse may be having a different "experience" completely. You'll also probably wonder when the two of you will ever have time alone again, and, when you do, if you'll have anything to talk about except the baby.

Your spouse may be having a different "experience" completely

New parents may miss—or even lose—old friends with whom they don't have time to socialize in the same way. Parents may find that the thrice-weekly work-out at the gym, or other hobbies or pursuits, done individually or together, are down the drain. Or, if one parent still pursues interests but the other parent sacrifices, the primary caregiver may be angry and jealous—and the other parent may be missing out on once-in-a-lifetime milestones with baby. Parents who had careers and were used to fast-paced environments and travel may feel cooped up or downright bored while staying at home.

Then there's a phenomenon called "The Baby Bomb," which basically means once the first baby is born, many marriages suffer. Sex may not resume soon or be the same for either or both partners. New roles as parents may take away from roles as attentive spouses. Rarely do two parents spend the same amount of time caring for the baby, or care for it in exactly the same way, so arguments and tensions ensue. It's no picnic.

It is also said that whatever problems a relationship has, those problems are heightened when a baby is added. Whether it's because your "parenting styles" differ, because you can't communicate worth beans, or just because you are tired and cranky, don't expect that you will always appear as that picture-perfect couple beaming proudly at their model baby. (In fact, take that picture-perfect couple, remove her makeup, draw in his growing beard, give them both dirty hair and bags under their eyes, turn that baby's grin into an open-mouthed scream, and you might have a more "normal" picture.) If your relationship problems are serious, however, perhaps now that you are parents you will seek the help you need.

> Don't expect that you will always appear as that picture-perfect couple beaming proudly at their model baby

All of that said, so what? Non-parents who read the above may decide never to be childbearing. But, honestly, for all the changes parenthood brings, it's amazing how much parents grow to love those little babes, and few parents would give back their child and regain their "old" lives.

The first baby during the first month is the hardest. By the time your child is four or five months old, that baby will be charming your socks off. And you may feel more comfortable hiring a babysitter so you can go out together, or you can meet for a lunch "date" while the baby is at day care.

> The first baby during the first month is the hardest

You may never "get back to normal," but you will develop a new normalcy that includes your child. In time, the really important activities will be added back into your lives. If you make an effort to do that, it can happen sooner than later.

Visitors

or "I'm coming to help"

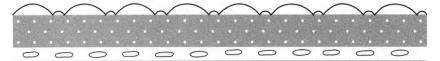

Most new parents probably would be hurt if no one showed any interest in seeing the new infant. And most people really do mean well.

But arriving home from the hospital tired, excited and anxious, all at once, with the new arrival can be exhausting.

First of all, either plan to ignore housekeeping and chores for awhile or arrange to get help, hired or otherwise, ahead of time. (A cluttered home with no refreshments can even serve to deter long-staying visitors.)

Secondly, visitors or phone calls do not have to be accepted.

How to get the rest you need

- Limit visits for tired mom (and probably dad, who may not have gone through physical labor but probably was up for the whole thing and is not getting his sleep, either). "Please - our visits are limited to 15 minutes for the time-being" could be posted on the door. Wear pajamas and a bathrobe to reinforce the idea.
- Whether napping or not, post a sign on the door, "New parent and baby napping til ___ o'clock." Don't answer the door until then.
- Unplug the phone.
- Leave a message on the answering machine with the news, turn the ringer on the phone off, and then let the answering machine kick in so the callers can get the information and you can call back at your convenience.
- Tell guests that you nap when the baby does, and you must excuse yourself. Then do it, even if guests must show themselves out.
- Don't offer refreshments, and don't apologize for it. In fact, suggest to guests who want to come near meal times that they bring a hot dish or fast food or swing by the deli on the way over.

Then suggest that "if they really wanted to help out" they could do the dishes before they leave.

- If everyone and his brother, including the runny-nosed kid down the street, want to hold and kiss your new baby, tell them, "Maybe you can hold and kiss the baby in a few weeks. He/She will be around for a long time and will appreciate your attention more when he/she is a little older."

"I'm coming to help"

NEW grandmothers/grandfathers/aunts/uncles/ cousins, etc., may want to come and "help out" when the new baby comes home from the hospital. If mom and dad and the "helper" get along well, if there's limited paternity leave or an unexpectedly difficult delivery, the help may be welcome and invaluable.

But too often such an announcement is unwelcome and such a visit creates more stress than adjusting to the new family life with the three of you.

This may be the first time that one or both parents will need to stand up to a well-meaning relative about their parenting preference. "We really appreciate your offer to help, but we need a little time to get the hang of this on our own. We'd like to wait awhile and set up a visit a little later on." Or, "If you really want to come this early, we'll be happy to reserve a room at a Bed-and-Breakfast in town and get you car rental information. We'd appreciate you staying there and keeping the visit short since we're really exhausted and we'd like some time alone."

This may be the first time that one or both parents will need to stand up to a well-meaning relative about their parenting preference

On the other hand, if someone does show up, don't be afraid to hand over a list: Walk the dog, vacuum, do laundry, dust, fix meals, grocery shop, wash the dishes, take the baby out for a stroll while you nap. After all, if they really are there to help, they won't be offended by such a list. Just make sure they get some time with baby, too, since the new baby, not doing your laundry, is the big attraction.

Legal stuff
"An ounce of prevention"

"We've got 20 minutes before he wakes up. So, what about a will?" This is an actual quote from an actual first-time parent. All of a sudden, legal documents and planning affect an innocent baby. And you don't have any time to get a shower, let alone take care of weighty matters.

Everyone leaves this stuff for last, but it shouldn't be put off. If possible, make whatever arrangements you can before the baby is born. You won't jinx the birth just because you wrote a will.

Will

A WILL is a good idea because it allows you, not a probate judge, to make important decisions about your estate. More importantly, a will establishes guardianship of your minor child, if something should happen to both parents. Simple wills don't have to be expensive, and may save your family a great deal of trouble and money. Sometimes attorneys offer will-writing seminars through continuing or community education departments of universities or school districts. State laws differ on what kind of wills are acceptable.

A will establishes guardianship of your minor child

Birth certificate

BIRTH CERTIFICATES are issued through the county in which the child was born (try the health, vital statistics or records departments). Your hospital usually handles this, but you may not get a certified copy unless you deal with the county (you may have to pay a fee). Inquire about the procedure, especially if you haven't selected a name for your baby before you leave the hospital. Baby will need a birth certificate to get a social security card, passport, enroll in school, get married or provide proof for many legal documents.

Social Security number

OK, THIS little girl or guy is not going to look for a job tomorrow. But for your taxes, to open a bank account for this baby and for other reasons, your baby soon needs a Social Security number.

Two forms of ID are required for the *baby*, an original or certified copy of the birth certificate and another. Since this child will have no driver's license, the federal folks suggest the baby's medical record number, crib card from the hospital bassinet, a prescription label, hospital ID band, etc.

ID is also needed for the parent signing the form for the child. A passport, government employee ID card, military records, insurance policy, clinic or doctor records or bills or a marriage record will work. No photocopies are accepted. The originals are returned.

Contact the Social Security Administration office nearest you for an application; you will mail it back to that office. The service is free; don't be taken in by offers to do this for you for a fee.

LIFE INSURANCE on the baby usually isn't necessary because the baby will have no income that needs to be replaced should the baby die. But if you would like insurance help with the baby's funeral and burial, you may want to buy some. Sometimes baby life insurance is so cheap—$10 a year or so for a $5,000 term policy through a parent's employer— it's hard to turn down.

Life insurance

Life insurance on the parents should be re-figured and increased now that you have a child to raise. How much to buy is a question only you can answer. Figure in the lost income of the spouse who dies, the cost of child care, post-secondary education, mortgage payments and other living expenses. For middle-income parents of a new baby who will attend college, don't be shocked to hear financial planners recommend $250,000-worth of insurance or more on each working parent. To figure out how much you need, and what type to buy, hire an independent financial planner, consult your tax accountant and/or research the subject through several financial-advice books.

Keep all legal documents in a safe deposit box at a bank or in a fireproof safe.

When you're all alone
Or feel that way

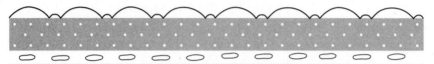

Need help? Need advice? Need to "ask a stupid question?"

First of all, you may not think this section is necessary. But if you've been sleep deprived and home with a colicky baby, you may not be thinking too clearly, through no fault of your own.

The heavy stuff first: If you are severely depressed and you feel you might hurt yourself or the baby or you want to leave the baby, call your obstetrician's office right away. Tell them this is an emergency, that you have severe post-partum depression and you need help immediately.

If you do not get a supportive answer, get out the yellow pages. Call a community mental health line and tell them the same thing. You may want to call **Depression After Delivery** Support Group, 215-295-3994, for a local chapter, or contact **Parents Anonymous** (in the yellow pages under "mental health", or 1-800-421-0353; or 213-410-9732). A "crisis nursery" also may be available in your area to take over baby care temporarily.

If the problem is not immediate or severe, many larger clinics and hospitals now offer support groups for post-partum depression. Ask for the parent education unit, the patient advocate's office, or work through your obstetrician's office.

Support and advice

YOUR PEDIATRICIAN'S office is a good source of information. Don't be afraid of bothering them. Find out about a "nurse line" or "help line" for after-hours calls.

You may wish to keep a list of friends, relatives or other parents near the phone to call for advice or information.

Some wonderful support and/or education groups for first-time parents exist, but you may have to do a little research.

- Ask your obstetrician and pediatrician.
- If you took a labor and delivery or child care class, call your educator.

- Ask if your state offers "early childhood and family education" through local school districts. If your district doesn't offer anything, call the state Department of Education and ask to talk to the Early Childhood specialist.
- Ask other new parents what they've found.
- Check to see if your church or others in the neighborhood sponsors such a group, knows of one, or is interested in starting one.

DON'T FEEL like there is a stupid baby-care question. If you don't know it, hundreds of others don't either.

For questions about clothing, call baby-specialty stores or baby departments. If they don't know the answer, ask them to look up the address or phone of the manufacturers of the particular item, and deal with the company directly.

Manufacturers of products and clothing often have a toll-free consumer information number printed on their item or its package. They can provide good information about baby food, baby laundry, baby diapers, etc., but remember they want to sell you more baby food, detergent or diapers, etc. If you don't have the company's toll-free number, call toll-free directory assistance, 1-800-555-1212.

If you need more specific information, call the reference desk at your local library (or drop in). The librarian can show you, for instance, a directory to associations and organizations, indexed by various topics, in case you don't have a specific name. If nothing else, the librarian may be able to tell you who else to call to ask who to call!

International Childbirth Education Association Bookcenter
Box 20048, Minneapolis, MN 55420
612-854-8660   1-800-624-4934
This association certifies instructors of labor/delivery/childcare classes, operates a Bookcenter and publishes a catalog, ICEA Bookmarks, four times a year. The comprehensive catalog includes book reviews and sales of popular or hard-to-find titles on many topics plus ICEA materials, ranging from a poster on how to breastfeed after a cesarean delivery to a plastic pelvis.

La Leche League International
Box 1209
9616 Minneapolis Ave., Franklin Park, IL 60131
708-451-1891
Breastfeeding support and supplies are for sale through a catalog that includes a large number of books and pamphlets on breastfeeding, as well as books on parenting. The group also can give information on local chapters and operates a breastfeeding helpline at 1-800-LA LECHE.

Nursing Mothers Counsel
P.O. Box 50063, Palo Alto, CA 94303
415-591-6688 to get phone numbers of regional chapters
Breastfeeding information sent and support and advice given over the phone by trained counselors who support the mother in whatever she chooses.

American Academy of Pediatrics
Publications Division
Box 927, Elk Grove Village, IL 60009
Brochures on such topics as choking prevention and infant first aid, care of the uncircumcised penis, vaccinations, diaper rash and choosing car seats. Write to get a list of member pediatricians in your area. Enclose a self-addressed, stamped envelope.

Consumer Product Safety Commission
Washington, D.C. 20207
Write for nursery equipment safety information, or call 1-800-638-2772 to hear taped information on safety and recalls.

Juvenile Products Manufacturers Association
Safety Certification Seal Program
Box 955, Marlton, NJ 08053
Send a self-addressed, stamped envelope for information on baby equipment safety standards.

Toy Manufacturers of America
P.O. Box 866
Madison Square Station, New York, NY 10159
Information can be sent to you about safe toys.

Buying the basics

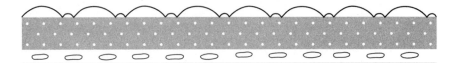

Before we talk about baby clothes, let's talk about *yours* (assuming you are the mom). This is not pretty, but it must be said: Don't wear anything that's not washable. You will soon feel you don't own a shirt that hasn't been spit-up on.

Moms who are anxious to get back into non-maternity clothes may be disappointed. It's usually at least a month, perhaps much longer, before the old stuff fits. Zahn's Law of Post-Partum Dressing: When you do reach your pre-pregnant weight, many of your old clothes won't fit anyway because your body has been...well... sort-of "redistributed." (But so what? You have this beautiful baby now, right? And someday those clothes can fit again.)

FIRST-TIME PARENTS often can go into a baby specialty store or the baby section of a department store and find a list of "everything your new baby needs." This list may fit on one 8-1/2 x 11-inch page, but it's probably printed in very small type. If you were to add up the cost of everything on that page, you might go into sticker shock. If you bought it all brand new, right there, right then, the store might honor you as "customer of the year." Other people might call you "sucker of the decade."

But all your baby *really* needs to come home from the hospital is diapers and a receiving blanket with a hood (or winter wear). If you're really strapped, you can get around the receiving blanket by using a soft towel. (The hospital may send baby off with a hat, t-shirt, or socks.)

Most parents probably will want to settle for something in the middle.

Even if you detest major, warehouse-like toy stores, spend a little time in their newborn departments. In addition to clothing, they probably will

Baby Stuff

Everything your baby needs to come home

have an overwhelming selection of nipples and cloth diapers and pacifiers from five or six manufacturers. It's not so overwhelming later, however, when you finally find one who makes reusable can covers that fit over a half-used can of formula, so you can get rid of that piece of plastic wrap secured with a rubber band. Meanwhile, you can buy one of each type of newborn pacifier and see which one (if any) your baby will like.

Below is information on baby clothes. In the next chapter there's a list of everything else that was recommended somewhere in this book.

SHOPPING FOR BABY clothes, primarily, opens a whole new world, sort of like when you lived in an apartment and you couldn't figure out, until you bought a house built in 1923, why giant building supply stores existed and who shopped there.

A "layette," for instance, is defined by one dictionary as "an outfit of clothing, bedding, etc., for a newborn child." You may receive a suggested "layette list" in the mail from some company who found out you were expecting or you can get one at a store or doctor's office. Remember, it's essentially advertising.

There are all sorts of manufacturer's terms for baby clothes. For example, one-piece T-shirts or outfits that snap at the crotch or up the legs may be called "onesies," "piluchos," "creepers," "layette gowns," "rompers," etc. Look carefully at the package and see if there's a drawing that shows exactly what the full-size garment looks like.

A NEWBORN has no idea what he or she is wearing. Clothing is made to appeal to parents and those shopping for gifts. It is important only that:
- baby be warm or cool enough,
- the garment has been laundered in baby detergent before wearing,
- there aren't irritating seams or pinching zippers, and

- it be easy to get on and off and open for diaper changes.

Of course, it should not be dangerous (strings at the neck, buttons that come off) or cause allergic reactions.

- Buy only machine-washable fabrics, unless you're either wealthy or the owner of a dry cleaner. (You'll be doing laundry every other day or so because of spit-up and diaper leaks.) Some parents prefer cotton or cotton-blends because it is natural, "breathes," and is less likely to cause allergic reactions or irritation.
- Snaps down *both* legs or some kind of easy-open access to the diaper is extremely helpful.
- The more snaps, the better. (For some reason, some manufacturers only have snaps or zippers down one leg, so the other leg has to be forced out, especially when the little darling is at capacity for that particular size.)
- Have front, not back, openings, so baby can see your face while you dress him or her, and you don't have to keep flipping baby over.
- Don't buy clothes with buttons, cutsey bows or other dangling features which can be pulled off and swallowed (even a five-month-old has amazing dexterity and strength when it comes to finding and removing these...).
- Avoid zippers that can pinch.
- Avoid cute appliqués on shirts or creepers that are unlined. They will scratch or rub on baby's tummy. Either sew a soft lining in yourself or dress baby with a t-shirt underneath.
- Lifting and carrying babies seems to twist their shirts and pant-legs up so bellies and legs are always exposed. To avoid constantly pulling shirts down to cover that tummy, buy one-piece outfits and t-shirts (for after the umbilical cord falls off). To avoid constantly pulling pant legs down to meet the socks, buy only outfits with "feet."

- Newborns don't like having shirts put on over their heads, so wrap-arounds or side-snaps will be much easier, even if that turtleneck is cute (newborns don't have necks, anyway, just folds of skin that collect lint!)..
- All "sleepwear" fabrics are supposed be flame-retardant. You'll need to find a baby laundry detergent, like Dreft, to preserve that retardant.
- Don't remove tags, unless they clearly irritate baby's neck. They'll be helpful in quickly finding the right-size garment and sorting wash, and important when giving away or selling garments at a garage sale or to a consignment shop.
- Go ahead, shop rummage and garage sales (sometimes mother's support groups for twins or other associations will have special large sales), thrift stores like Goodwill and consignment shops. The little creeper that's $15.95 in the store may only be 50 cents or $1 when it's slightly used, and you'll need to launder both the new and used one before your baby can wear it, anyway. Stained shirts or creepers can be hidden under sweatshirts. Unlike cribs, strollers and car seats, there's usually not a recall concern on clothing.
- Likewise, accept (even solicit!) all hand-me-downs gracefully, at least for now.

Sizes   **"Newborn" size** (sometimes listed as "0") will fit only for about a month or less (they go to about 10 pounds). Those little sizes are really cute. But don't buy many, if any, newborn clothes since they just don't last long—maybe a month or two. Also, if you have a 10-pound baby (bless you!), newborn size might not fit at all.

Newborns can come home in and spend their first month in clothes marked "small" or "6 months" sizes. Bigger doesn't hurt. Roll up the sleeves, or leave them down to keep hands warm and baby from scratching himself or herself. Items like kimono gowns, which have no feet, won't be outgrown as quickly as fitted outfits.

Here's where it gets confusing. "Small," "medium" and "large" are relative terms depending on the manufacturer's definition. Look for pounds on the tags, which are much more accurate. Even then, smalls may run 14-18 pounds, 13-17, 12-17, 13-16 and 15-18, depending on the company. Mediums may cover an even wider range, 17-21 or 19-26. (No, the author doesn't know what you do if all your baby's clothes are for 13-16 pounds or 19-26 and your baby weighs 17 or 18...)

Sizes also come in months: 0 (newborn), 2 or 3 (sometimes), 6, 9, 12, 18 and 24. But they're not accurate. *In the beginning, double your baby's age to find the right size.* A three-month old, then, usually would wear a 6-month size *or bigger*. However, just when you think you have this figured out, you'll find your 12-month-old actually wears a 12-month size from one manufacturer.

Here's how one major manufacturer figures it:

- 3-6 months size fits 11-14 pounds, 22-24 inches in height.
- 6-9 months fits 14.5-18 pounds, 25-27 inches.
- 12 months fits 18.5-23 pounds, 27.5-30.5 inches.
- 18 months fits 23.5-26 pounds, 31-33 inches.
- 24 months fits 26.5-28 pounds, 33.5-35.5 inches.

Figure that an 8-pound baby (at the larger end of the usual newborn weight range) might be 20 or 21 inches long. So that baby might be in this clothing company's 3-6 month clothing size range by two months old, and could well have outgrown that size by four months old.

Shopping checklists

Basic clothing, size 6 months or "small"

Suggested numbers of clothing or outfits should just get you started. Because of diaper leaks, spit up and other hazards, you may change a newborn's clothing six times a day. Based on these numbers, you will need to do laundry every other or every third day, if not every day. To stretch out laundry times (you don't want to wait too long with poopy or stained clothes, though), buy additional items.

This list also will allow you a couple weeks to form your own preferences. You and your baby may love or hate the kimonos, for instance. Following this list will mean you haven't sunk a huge investment into any one item. (Shop garage sales, consignment shops and thrift stores. Just wash everything well in baby detergent, which you need to do with brand-new items, anyway.)

To start

__ **3-6 cotton T-shirts**, long or short-sleeved, or both, with snap front-openings
Buy short or long-sleeved depending on the season(s). Buy ones with front-openings; babies hate having shirts put on over their heads.

T-shirts along with a diaper are the cheapest, easiest lounge-about clothes for newborns. They offer protection for delicate skin against cheap metal snaps on creeper/sleeper outfits (if baby is allergic to this metal, it may leave a snap-sized ring on baby's tummy that looks like ringworm). Also, T-shirts are great until the umbilical cord falls off because they can be folded up and the diaper folded down to avoid irritating the cord.

The down-side is they often get bunched up under baby's arms, requiring near-constant attention to keep tummy warm and baby comfortable, more of an issue for winter babies. For the months after the cord falls off, buy larger-size one-piece t-shirts that have snaps at the crotch—there's no ride-up problem. But winter babies can still use these to wear under one-piece outfits.

__ **60-100 Diapers**, or "diaper starter kit," disposable, cloth or through a home-delivered diaper service (see description of types, page 59).

Plan to go through six to 12 a day, but some babies use up to 20. Start with 60-100 for the first five days or so of diaper service; perhaps 40 if home-laundering.

If you are using traditional cloth, also buy:

— **pins, waterproof pants or diaper covers.**

If you are using disposables, also buy:

— *1 dozen cloth diapers* for use as lap or shoulder pads, changing pads, to cut up for emergency nursing pads, or great eyeglass wipers and window washing cloths later.

— **1 package diaper pins or 1 roll masking tape** to reclose a diaper after the sticky tape no longer sticks (an occasional problem)

— 4-6 sleeper/romper/creeper one-piece outfits

These may be long or short-sleeved, with or without feet, depending on the season. Baby can wear these around the clock; there's no need for pajamas (dressing and undressing at this age just bugs them). Because these can be cute, you may get them as gifts. Once you know what types you like, buy several more in "medium" size.

Make sure there are snaps *as far down both legs as possible.* (Manufacturers who make these with snaps a little ways down one leg, for example, or down both legs but then have cuffs on the bottom at the ankles, should be taken out and given 50 lashes with a wet diaper.) Without snaps all the way down both legs, you end up cramming one leg and feet in and out. (Zippers hardly ever go down both legs and can sometimes pinch tender baby skin, or be uncomfortable to lie on, if baby sleeps stomach down.)

Buy footed ones for all but the hottest weather (baby can wear just a diaper and T-shirt then). Non-footed ones require socks, and the pant legs always ride up every time baby moves or is picked up, leaving a nasty sock-pant gap (and for some reason, baby socks don't go high up on the leg).

Avoid unlined appliqués which will scratch baby's tummy. If an outfit has an appliqué, sew in a soft lining or make sure baby wears a t-shirt underneath.

— 2-4 kimono-type gowns

These one-size-fits-all gowns (more like bags with arms) have no legs in them, just a drawstring or snaps at the bottom, easy for diaper changes. But they may ride up under the arms like T-shirts. Newer model ones (sometimes called "after bath" gowns because they have a hood to keep the wet head warm) have a covered zipper down the front and are sewn shut at the bottom—great for the riding up problem, but harder for diaper changes.

_ 3-6 pairs of socks

"Booties" with formed feet like slippers or shoes aren't necessary and socks stay on better. Check elastic to make sure it won't be too tight. Weight depends on the season; in winter, put them on under the "feet" in one-piece outfits. Hints: Buy all one color style so the "lost" one doesn't mean its mate is doomed to never being worn again. White is fine since these babies don't walk on them and get them dirty. These often come in packages of three pairs; buy only a few small and several 9-18 month sizes as the elastic often is tight on the smaller ones, which pinches fat baby legs.

_ 2-3 newborn hats

Weight should depend on the season; buy sunhats for summer babies, warmer caps for winter babies (if you're buying wool, make sure it has a non-scratching cotton lining). Buy at least two because you'll misplace one.

Other basics

_ 4-6 receiving blankets, 2-3 hooded

Receiving blankets come in different sizes, materials and with/ without a hood in the corner. You'll use them for several months, possibly years.

Hooded blankets are good for keeping body heat in after a shampooing, as well as for outside wear.

Receiving blankets often are used to tightly swaddle a fussy infant and put him/her to sleep; the theory is being wrapped feels secure, like the womb. The baby can "wear" its swaddling blanket anytime, except during diaper changes.

A rolled blanket or two on each side of the head or around the head can stabilize the baby's neck and head in a car seat, stroller or swing.

The baby can sleep on its side if one blanket is rolled and placed behind its back, neck and head, another rolled and placed against its tummy (but well away from its face).

In a pinch, an older (or less attractive) blanket can do as a changing pad or as a shoulder or lap pad for burping, or as a lap pad/clothing protector while holding or feeding the baby.

As baby grows, use the rectangular flannel ones as teething pads spread across the crib and tucked in at both sides. Baby will drool while sleeping and these can be changed easily and quickly. Figuring in naps and overnight, you may use three or four of these a day.

__ 0-2 bibs

Newborns don't drool and don't slobber solid food down their chins. But bottles do leak and milk may run down their chins, and spit-up runs down chins and everything else. A bib could be attached for feeding time, but most parents just put a clean cloth diaper or rag under the baby's chin while feeding and on their shoulder for burping.

You'll need bibs for drooling as early as three months and for solid food as early as four or five months; drool bibs (they look like miniature bibs) can be purchased used but food bibs (they cover almost head to toe, or should) will be heavily stained. Hint: Don't buy any that tie or have button-closures as they just take too long to get on and off. Look for bibs with snaps, especially snaps in two or three places so the neck opening can be expanded as baby does.

__ **Mittens, snowsuit/bunting, other winter gear** for babies born in the fall, winter or spring, depending on your geographical location. A "baby bag" with legs but no sleeves is perfect for easy dressing outerwear (the legs allow the "bag" to be strapped into a car seat, but the baby can't do anything with his or her arms anyhow, so keep them tucked in).

__ **Diaper bag** or old flight carry-on bag, gym bag or other bottomless pit. (See section on Diapers/Diaper bag to figure out what will go in there. You'll need it for outings, though.)

__ **Chest of drawers** or shelves, or somewhere to put this stuff.

__ Nursery intercom/monitor

This allows parents to leave the room and hear the baby in other parts of the house or in the yard if baby's awake. Buy one with two channels to reduce the chances of hearing the neighbor's baby on your monitor. Some now come with two-way systems, like intercoms, so a parent can talk back through the monitor. That's handy when one parent needs help or supplies in the nursery and the other parent is downstairs, out of ear-shot.

— **Car seat** specifically designed for an infant (see page 84); it's the law.

— **Smoke detector for nursery.**

Optional, or to purchase later

— **1-2 sweaters or jackets**
Weight should depend on the season. Receiving blankets may substitute for this.

— **Lamp(s), crib light, nightlights** or **dimmer switch on overhead light**
Then parents don't have to turn on the bright overhead light everytime they come in to check on the sleeping baby. (Babies aren't afraid of the dark, and turning on the light probably won't wake the baby, but it can irritate the sleepy parents. But you do want to keep nighttime feedings dark so your baby doesn't wake right up to play all night.)

— **2-4 baby-sized washcloths**
These are much easier to use than adult-sized washcloths on tiny baby body parts, and they can be used for months or years.

Complete shopping list of everything mentioned in this book

(in addition to items mentioned above)

Basic items recommended before bringing baby home :

— **Bassinet, cradle, padded laundry basket** or **padded dresser drawer** for sleeping (page 9)

— **Waterproof changing pad,** often found in diaper bag, or use clean diapers or blankets (pages 50, 55)

— **Changing table** at home where baby's diapers will be changed (page 49)

— **Rubbing alcohol** for cleaning umbilical cord (pages 69, 72, 89)

— **Sterile cotton balls** for cleaning eyes, bottom, **swabs** for umbilical cord care (pages 51, 69, 72, 89)

If you buy a changing table, make sure it has a railing around the pad. A safety strap should be used, too.

— **Petroleum jelly** or prescribed ointment for circumcision care (pages 53, 70, 72, 89)

— **Baby laundry detergent** to wash everything baby wears, sleeps on, is wrapped in or touches (page 79)

— **2-4 Pacifiers,** silicone or vinyl, orthodontic or newborn-sized, air holes around the shield, different shapes to suit baby's preference, if you opt to use them (pages 28, 87)

— **Neck support pillow** or rolled-up towel or blankets, to be used in cradle, swing, stroller and car seat (pages 20, 63, 86)

For use with home-laundered cloth diapers:

— **Soaking pail** (page 52)

— **Chlorine bleach** (page 80)

— **Rubber gloves** or diaper tongs for rinsing diapers in the toilet (page 52)

For use with disposable diapers:
___ **Diaper pail**, lined with a plastic bag, foot-pedal preferred (pages 51, 55)

Nice to have before bringing baby home, or soon thereafter:

___ **Rocking chair** for nursing, calming, cooing (page 11)
___ **Baby-carrier seat** on a metal frame for lounging, snoozing (page 12)
___ **Front pack or baby sling** for carrying a newborn but leaving parent's hands free (page 15)
___ **Swing**, wind-up or electric, preferably with at least a 15-minute timer, with cradle or seat and head/neck support, for use only with very fussy baby (pages 20, 63)
___ **Stroller**, which can recline all the way to flat, not umbrella type for newborn (page 86)
___ **Vacuum cleaner** to soothe a crying baby—the noise, not the suction (page 19)
___ Mild **baby soap** or **shampoo** (pages 68, 74, 89)
___ **Blunt-end nail scissors** (pages 68, 90)
___ **Baby comb** and **brush** (pages 68, 90)
___ **Bulb aspirator** for suctioning the nose and mouth (pages 68, 90)
___ **Baby-sized bathtub** or **giant, baby-sized sponge** or large towel for the bottom of the sink or tub where baby will be bathed once umbilical cord has fallen off and circumcision has healed (page 74)
___ **Digital thermometer** for rectal and under-arm use (page 82)
___ **Lubricating jelly** for rectal thermometer (and sexual interludes, if there are any) (page 83 for rectal use, page 97 for mention about sex)
___ **Witch hazel** for relief of mom's episiotomy and hemorrhoid discomfort (page 94)
___ **Sanitary napkins** for lochia discharge (and to cut up and use as nursing pads, in a pinch) (page 95)
___ **Supportive bra** for non-nursing moms in pain when milk comes in (page 96)

Optional, or to be purchased later:

___ **Crib** and maybe also bumper pad, crib sheets, waterproof mattress cover, dust ruffle (pages 8, 9, 86, 87)
___ **Infant massage books** or **videos** (pages 19, 66)
___ **Hot water bottle** to soothe baby (pages 21)

___ **Crib shaker** for soothing colicky babies (very optional; page 24)

___ **Noisy fan** or **air conditioner** (page 19)

___ **Soothing music** or **radio** for nursery, to entertain or calm baby (page 19)

___ **Baking soda** for use in bathtub to soothe diaper rash or prickly heat (pages 76, 77) and to clean spit-up stains (page 48)

___ **Black-and-white mobiles or designs** (page 64 and see below)

___ **Play "gym"** with dangling toys and mirrors (page 64)

___ **Baby toys like rattles or rings or plastic people or animals** (page 64)

___ **Mosquito netting** (page 78)

___ **Room humidifier** or **vaporizer** (page 85)

Baby toys

Baby toys for newborns may be hard to find since many department or discount stores don't carry them.

Some sources of "toys" like black-and-white mobiles and designs for newborns are specialty kids toy stores, specialty baby stores, and sometimes shops in children's or natural history museums that carry educational toys.

While there are dozens of catalogs that carry products for older kids, a few which carry mobiles, etc., for infants are (listed alphabetically):

- Constructive Playthings (catalog), 1227 E. 119th St., Grandview, MO 64030; 1-800-832-0572.
- The Livonia Catalog, 306 Hebron St., Hendersonville, NC 28739; 1-800-543-8566.
- One Step Ahead (catalog), 950 Northshore Dr., Lake Bluff, IL 60044; 1-800-950-5120
- The Right Start Catalog, Right Start Plaza, 5334 Sterling Center Drive, Westlake Village, CA 91361; 1-800-LITTLE 1 (548-8531).

These catalogs also have nifty toys, safety accessories and unique convenience items; gift certificates available. Also:

- Growing Child, 22 N. Second Street, Lafayette, IN 47902-0620; 1-800-927-7289. This monthly newsletter also sells educational products. The newsletter gives excellent information on what baby should be doing each month and how parents can provide stimulation.

Feeding supplies for breastfeeding

Basic items recommended before bringing baby home :

___ **Nursing pads** (purchased or cut-up cloth or disposable diapers or sanitary pads, or cotton handkerchiefs, laundered well, page 38)

___ **A few baby bottles** (page 38)

— A can of formula for emergencies (page 39)
— A good reference book on breastfeeding (page 39)

Nice to have before bringing baby home, or soon after:
— Plastic refrigerator container for storing milk (page 37)
— 1-3 Nursing bras (page 38)

Optional, or to be purchased later:
— Breast pump, electric, battery-operated or manual *{Note: some mothers consider this a necessity}* (page 39)
— Nursing gowns, shirts, night shirts or pajamas (page 39)

Feeding supplies for bottlefeeding

Basic items recommended before bringing baby home :
— 6-10 bottles, four or eight-ounce size, glass, plastic or "disposable nurser" with disposable liners, or a nursing "starter kit" (pages 42, 46)
— 2-4 extra nipples, preferably silicone or vinyl "orthodontic" or newborn to fit the bottles, above (page 46)
— A few cans of formula, powder, concentrate or ready-to-use (pages 41, 46)
— Refrigerator container used only to mix and store formula (pages 42, 44)
— Bottle brush, if not using disposable liners (page 46)

Nice to have before bringing baby home, or soon thereafter:
— Bottle caps or lids to fit the bottles, above (page 46)

Optional, or to be purchased later:
— Cases of formula, the type your baby prefers and your pediatrician okays (page 41)
— New can opener used exclusively for opening canned formula (page 46)
— Ice chest to hold prepared bottles in the bedroom (page 44)
— Hot pot or carafe filled with hot or sterilized water to mix bottles during the night (page 44)
— Electric bottlewarmer, though most parents/babies won't wait for these to work (page 47)
— Electric bottle sterilizer if you insist on sanitary bottles (page 47)
— More bottles in a size, shape or decoration you or baby prefer (page 47)
— Juice nipples or nipples for older babies (page 47)

128

Advice from new parents

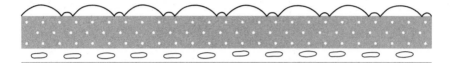

A number of first-time parents were asked, "If you could pass on a bit of advice or information to new parents about the first few weeks and caring for their newborn, what would it be?" Here are their responses:

"The first few weeks are tough. Expect to be tired and feel over-whelmed. If you expect it to be tough in the beginning, you won't be in for such a shock when it happens."   -First-time Mom

"Nurture 'em both — Mom and the baby. Sleep the way they do, whenever you can."   -First-time Dad

"New moms should take naps. I never did and I was always tired. The dishes can wait."   -First-time Mom

"It will be better later! The first two months are the worst."
                    -First-time Mom

"Take as much time from work as you can afford to. You've produced a *person* and it's someone you need to get to know."
                    -First-time Mom

"Much easier said than done, but *relax*. Try to get lots of sleep. Hold your baby a *lot*. Talk to it, read to it. Keep it in the bedroom with you at least the first two or three weeks. It reduces anxiety, I think."
                    -First-time Mom

"Even if it costs you, take as much time off as you can. You can make the money later — you can't recapture that time, ever."
                    -First-time Dad

"You might not think you'll like your own baby, and it might take awhile. But it's amazing how much you don't just *like* them but *love* them. And it grows as they do."   -First-time Mom

"If possible, have an experienced parent spend the first few days with you, a friend or parent."   -First-time Dad

"It's important to have time together, alone, for you three — mom, dad, baby as a new family. If visitors create stress, just say no."
                                                                       -First-time Mom

"You made this baby and have already been raising them for nine months. You know what's best for that baby. Listen to advice, but your gut feelings will tell you what to do."   -First-time Mom

"Be prepared for a shock. It's wonderful being a parent, but there's a lot of big adjustments to make."   -First-time Mom

"Don't expect bliss that first month. There's a lot to learn, a lot to do in caring for a newborn. It's hard, but it's not awful — I found I *liked* it, which surprised the hell out of me."   -First-time Mom

"Those snaps on the nighties at 4 a.m., don't expect to get them snapped right."   -First-time Dad

"Express some milk and get Baby used to taking a bottle once in awhile so Dad can help feed Baby and so you can get a sitter once in awhile."
                                                                       -First-time Mom

"Don't wear anything that isn't washable. Don't let friends or relatives wearing dry-clean-only clothes hold the baby unless you are prepared to pay the cleaning bill."   -First-time Mom

"Make no special social plans (but have people over if you feel like it). Keep *all* obligations to a minimum. Your focus is on the baby."
                                                                       -First-time Mom

"Take turns getting out of the house or at least away from the baby to relax. The nicest thing my husband did for me was to give me an hour and a half to myself when he came home from work — to take a bath, go out, or just hide for awhile."   -First-time Mom

"Buy your equipment in advance, take prenatal classes, get a book like Dr. Spock, take off more vacation time than 2 days."
                                                                       -First-time Dad

"Have a sense of humor. Seriously, folks, I don't know how people can survive as parents if they can't laugh about stuff like meconium."

-First-time Mom

"Don't try to do everything yourself. Dads can help—they know stuff, too." -First-time Mom

"Relax a bit about it. Find other parents to talk to. And take pictures — lots of them!" -First-time Mom

"Have low expectations for trying to do anything except baby care. It's amazing how little you'll get done, and it'll be frustrating. But house-cleaning and cooking don't matter. Learning to care for your new one does." -First-time Mom

"Don't worry about handling your baby. Follow your instincts."

-First-time Dad

"Go with the flow! Get support from other moms, but only take advice seriously from one/your closest friend/relative. Be as (physically) fit as you can." -First-time Mom

"Be well prepared at home prior to birth. Have enough supplies so that you do nothing but care for the baby for the first week. Have family/ parental help close by, or close friends." -First-time Dad

"I didn't expect problems with breastfeeding. No one said that whatever you do, you'll get sore, and it wasn't a wonderful, easy, or natural experience from Day 1. The pediatrician was hopeless and demotivating —other mums and close friends were great. It all took much longer than I imagined—almost six weeks, I'd say, to really 'work.'"

-First-time Mom

"Get a digital thermometer." -First-time Mom

"Don't burp baby too enthusiastically." -First-time Dad

The first 30 days

A new mom's diary of the first month

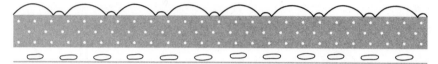

My mother is going to hate when I say this (and perhaps others will, too), but, now that I look back, bringing our son home from the hospital was very much like bringing our new puppy home from the Humane Society.

OK, there were some major differences: Kirby was 12 weeks old, Jay was 4 days old. Kirby had four legs, Jay had two. Kirby had fur, Jay had some hair, etc.

But my point is, neither one of them knew what the hell was going on. And neither did we. We had never been puppy parents or baby parents before (though I highly recommend going the pet route first, as caring for another live being is a good segue into human parenthood, despite what my mother might think).

Kirby had her tail between her legs, scared out of her little puppy mind, for what seemed like weeks. She didn't know where she could eat, sleep, pee, etc., and we were constantly patrolling to make sure she was doing all of the above in the right places at the right time. Big stress on both sides. Bright dog though she was, it seemed like it took forever, six months maybe, before she knew the rules and felt at home.

It took about six weeks with the baby, and was a lot easier on the carpet. Not that he knew any rules after six weeks, just that he seemed to be more aware, less fetal and fragile (and he was a strapping 8 pounds, 2 ounces at birth).

When you think about it, birth is a big deal on his end, too.

And after about six weeks, I seemed to feel more comfortable with him, like he was part of the family, like I didn't have to be afraid of him and his irrationality (maybe because he didn't seem so irrational, but more predictable).

8/24 - Saturday
Jay Edward Miller was born healthy by c-section at 11:20 a.m., after 16 hours of labor at the hospital. Heard him cry first, then an awkward sideways glance (can't really see well without glasses). Both my arms are flung out and strapped down. Jim went to the nursery with him, then home to make phone

calls. I went to the recovery room for two hours, was in and out of consciousness.

In my room in the evening, Mary the Nurse and another nurse ask me to sit up and walk. There is a catheter and an IV to contend with, and this is a major procedure. I scooted over to the edge of the bed, put my feet on the floor, stood up and felt like all my guts were going to spill out and hit the floor. Mary asked if I wanted to walk to the bathroom or get back in bed. I said, "Get back in bed." This was major surgery.

8/25 - Sunday
Staples in incision are metal.

I have no voice from puking during labor.

I can't believe how little I can do and how much it hurts.

Robert (brother-in-law) and his girlfriend visit.

I have never seen people so concerned about flatulence. "Once you pass gas, you can have real food," the nurse says. At 7:30 p.m., I buzz the nurse and tell her to mark my chart. The midwife reminds us we will have to choose a method of birth control. A cruel joke.

8/26-Monday
Doctor says I am supposed to have a suppository and shower today.

Jay had circumcision in the morning, which Jim watched, and said wasn't too awful. Jay had blood drawn from his foot for PKU test, and he screamed, then puked. Jim said Jay cried more from that than getting shot for circumcision or circumcision itself.

Jim was gone from 1 to 5 or 5:30, so I slept with Jay, who slept on my chest. I couldn't get out of bed by myself, so I got the nurse to help me get up to go to the bathroom.

Jay puked on Patrice while she visited. I swell up like crazy while talking to Beth, when she visited.

My sister-in-law, who also had a long labor and then a c-section, called and said that during hard labor "any Tom, Dick or Harry who comes up the stairwell might as well stick his hand up your crotch — everyone else has!" I pass the phone to Jim, since laughing hurts my belly so much.

By 9 p.m., I still have not had either shower or BM. I am discouraged at the idea of getting up the step into the shower, which is not hand-held. My milk is coming in, and my breasts are sagging. I take a sponge bath. We take Jay to the nursery at 12 midnight and I take a stool softener.

I don't want more visitors. I cry about swelling, the pain, my boobs, about not getting better, and not being ready to go home.

8/27 - Tuesday

I am up about 7:30 for the BM. "My," I say out loud, then stop myself from painful laughing, when I realize it is as big as Jay. (At least I delivered it normally.)

Bad gas today. Shortness of breath from bloating.

I give Jay a bath with Jim's help. For the first time, I've really been able to examine his body and see my little guy. I change my first diaper. I didn't get the leg of the diaper around his leg and scrotum, and found myself saying, "Help me!"

First day I can get in and out of bed by myself. A good day.

At night, I'm depressed I'm not getting better, not participating in baby care — all I can do is hold him and feed him while I'm lying down. At 4:30 a.m., a night nurse takes my vitals while I'm sitting on the toilet, wishing I could pass gas. She tells me this is normal, don't worry. After major surgery, patients have a bad day about three or four days later, where they are weepy and depressed, regardless of type of surgery or reason for it. How come nobody clued me in on that until now?

8/28-Wednesday

We went down to the nursery to get Jay at 7 a.m. I could hear him cry down the hall — it made my heart beat a little faster and my pathetic steps move a little quicker. He was in the swing, screaming, and the nurse was cranking it up again. Why, if he's the only baby in the nursery, was he in the swing? And why was he, as a newborn, in that swing, anyway?

I feel better today. We got home from the hospital. My brother, sister-in-law and two nieces are there but they leave blessedly soon. Both Jay and Mom are tired. I change a diaper. Somewhere along the line, perhaps when Jim "abandoned" us on Sunday and left us alone for four hours, I absolutely fell in love with this baby.

8/29 - Thursday

This afternoon, after a feeding, I began singing old sappy camp songs. Jay is a most appreciative audience. You would have thought I was Barbra Streisand doing her greatest hits.

Jim is carrying him around the house, swaddling and wrapping him in the flash of an eye, like an old pro. I feel I'm just getting started. It still hurts to carry him in front. I can't burp him well. I did two diaper changes today, and it was no big deal by the second. I'm still very awkward at picking him up — it's the first day I really have.

Today, Jay is turning toward my breast when I bottlefeed him. He has been doing that but it bothers me today. (Does he smell the milk or what?) I'm still engorged but the milk is on its way out. Guilt about that? I am worried that all he wants me for is a bottle and an occasional tune, but when he finally falls asleep gazing at me, I feel more confident. I can hold him on a pillow with the pillow on my stomach.

I am up all night every two or three hours with water flushing itself out. I forgot my bladder ever held so much. My hands and fingers look almost as if I could wear my wedding ring again. But my ankles, feet and boobs are still swollen.

I really noticed the pupils in Jay's eyes for the first time.

In the shower, I realize how different this birth has been from what I envisioned. I am shaved where I didn't want to be, and there is body hair where I normally would have shaved by now. Every step, every reach is still more difficult than being 9-plus months pregnant. Only that sweet, healthy little boy downstairs has made this outcome OK.

During a diaper change, I notice how there is this sort-of curdy poop that is not that hard to clean up. "Yeah," Jim said, "it's like it doesn't really stick to his butt. Now that meconium, *that* stuck to his butt." It was like tar, and the hospital had given these ridiculously thin wipe things to clean it off with.

Jay continues his molt. It was a hot day, and the perspiration in the folds of his arms and on his face necessitates a sponge bath. It was much quicker than in the hospital.

The plastic ring on his weenie has started to fall off. I want to keep this, perhaps to blackmail him with in the future. (It is so little, how can those doctors do a good job?)

The stroller ride down the block, Jim reports, seems to fascinate him.

It surprises me he puts up with as much T-shirts-wrapped-around-his-armpit-and-chest, bundle-of-blanket, as he does — I still feel very awkward about handling him, as he doesn't come in one neat little bundle except immediately after wrapping him.

Once over-feeding him has resulted in a semi-projectile puke. I'm now trying to "entertain" or engage him some other way (besides feeding), as I can physically.

I'm surprised how often I check him to see if he's too hot, too cold, has spit up, is the blanket in his face, or ?

8/30 - Friday
Jay's plastic penis ring came off in the 3 a.m. diaper change.

Tried to switch him over to powdered formula today. He puked on me twice, once on Jim. Big mistake — I made one bottle up when he was hungry. All the shaking required to dissolve the powder made it nothing but bubbles. He was up and fussy for two hours this afternoon.

I noticed some diaper rash on his right thigh, so I decided to let him have some air. I put a waterproof pad on the couch. Of course, he sprayed a nice little fountain on me, the blanket and a couple drops on the couch before I got the diaper over his penis.

I am feeling better — less pain and more mobile. I took a shower. My breasts are now pre-pregnant size and still shrinking. I was sad, somehow, they never got used for their intended purpose, after hauling them around for all these years.

One of the best things is changing the diaper *after* feeding him. He's all groggy and can't protest too much.

Funny thing. Neither of us miss work, or even thinks of it, and we are perfectly happy to hang around the house with our boy.

8/31 - Saturday (not that it makes any difference what day it is)
He sprayed me and my PJs at the midnight diaper change.

At 9 a.m., when I got up, Jim announced he had been peed on twice since 3 a.m. The little guy has transformed a simple diaper change into an art form.

Jim has the 3-9 a.m. shift. He goes to bed at 9 or 10, last night for the first time since surgery in bed with me. I went to sleep at about the same time, but I still wake at nearly every moan and coo. Jim can sleep through anything, including me getting up with the baby, and feeding him — so I get up until 3 or so and then I get Jim up. He takes the baby downstairs and simply stays up (Jim also needs very little sleep).

Jay's fairly regular schedule — up for 1 to 2 hours, sleep for 1 to 3 hours — has dissolved. He was up for four hours or so in the late afternoon/ evening, went for a stroller ride and had a shampoo, both of which were upsetting.

The Routine: Cries, up, has 1/3 to 1/2 bottle, burp, 1/3 to 1/2 more bottle, burp, may fall asleep on shoulder (loves that position), may take the rest of bottle, diaper change/cord clean, look at me lovingly or cuddles on chest until falls back asleep.

New Addition: Stays awake, wants to be walked around, may puke extra milk or have gas, may want pacifier or more milk.

I'm down 28 pounds, and I only gained 31 or so. My 41-inch waist is now 33 inches. It's mostly due to diet (after, of course, all that flushing out a couple days ago of water-weight gain) as my intestines still are not functioning properly and I must be careful about what I eat.

Lisa calls from Seattle and tells a similar story of labor and c-section two years ago with her boy. "Let me warn you about the abdominal surgery producing intestinal gas," she says too late. "I broke the towel rack in the downstairs bathroom" by gripping it so hard because of the pain. Curious the nurses don't offer anything but laxatives, stool softeners or suppositories. Haven't these people heard of a $1.89 supply of Maalox? Tums, Rolaids, Alka Seltzer, anything? Ginger ale is what I got.

My shortest time for a two-ounce feeding, burping and changing was 40 minutes.

Our "bundle of joy." I won't agree it is always is a bundle of joy, but they always are a bundle of something. Sometimes it's pee and poop. Nobody said, though, they they could be a warm, sweet-smelling cuddler sleeping on your shoulder or chest.

I like kimonos. They give easy access to his diaper. There's room and air in there by his legs, yet they're enclosed. T-shirts tend to get wrapped around his armpits, leaving his middle exposed and all this material bunched up near his neck.

We are at less than four clothing changes a day. Changes are due to spit-up. Is it possible to wear one outfit all day?

9/1 - Sunday

Jay is "getting" eyebrows.

Pictures came from our hospital stay. His head is sort of lopsided in the nursery shots, evidence that he just wasn't making it through the pelvis.

I noticed how much more confident, or less awkward, I feel about handling him. Placing him up for a burp, for instance, isn't so major a deal (though some of that is because I can lift better), knowing that he *will* eventually burp, laying him down for a diaper change, *he* seems more accustomed to it, too. It has been good not to have been able to go anywhere or do anything this first week, so the little tasks could be partially mastered and some confidence built.

Took him to the neighbors for a Labor Day cookout.

He is starting to stay awake and interact more now at some feedings. We purposely kept him up and withheld the last one ounce of bottle until 10:30, trying to move the night feeding times back.

I went through the whole day with no nap!

9/3 - Tuesday

Sleep is all screwed up. We all slept from about 11:45 p.m. - 2 a.m., then Jay and Jim went back to sleep and I didn't, until after 4. Got up at 10. How will this work when Jim goes back to work?

Jay had his first trip to Toys 'R Us and slept through the whole thing.

Carpal tunnel syndrome (actually D'Quervain's Disease) is back (I had it during pregnancy), especially during burping the baby.

9/4 - Wednesday
I think the first 10 days or so are designed to acclimate new parents to pee, poop and puke, the Three Ps. Last night, after Letterman, Jay puked up a feeding that slimed me, a pillow, top and bottom sheets we were sitting on, and through to the mattress pad. At lunch, he barfed all over himself and my shirt, and mopping that up nearly made me gag for the first time. Amazing how two ounces of milk turns into 1-1/2 gallons when spewed out in a millisecond by darling-baby-turned-demon.

On the other hand, I got a tremendous laugh when I was singing him the theme from the "Beverly Hillbillies." Right when I sang, "Up from the ground came a bubblin' crude," there was, indeed, "a bubblin' crude" heard loud and clear in his diaper.

Jim and I took him in to Jim's office at lunch. He was fast asleep in his car seat when Jim carried him in, and there was an audible, "Awwwww," from the women gathered at the lunch table (the three men said nothing). Four women quickly lined up to hold the sleeping cutie pie (one man refused, the two others looked away). Jim is unembarrassed about being the proud father.

9/5 - Thursday
Jay's face looks broader, older, already. He wasn't born yesterday, you know.

He seems to cry more, harder, at diaper changes and when hungry.

Today's puke was in front of the neighbors, who had fed and held him.

Our first sexist comments came today from middle-aged folks. One (from a male) made some remark to Jim to the effect of "you got the boy you really wanted." Actually, I was the one who was hoping for a boy, and believed I was carrying one. The other comment (from a female) was about "Jim getting an education in baby care." Ha! As the oldest of 10, this is like riding a bike to him. I am the one getting the first-time education.

I spent some time digging out pre-maternity clothes. I have mixed feelings. It will be good to have a "new" wardrobe but I will be able to wear nothing "good" that cannot withstand spit-up abuse for a long time.

Once while Jay was napping I pulled back the receiving blanket to find beads of perspiration on his head. Oh, guilt pangs of the bad baby mom! I had overwrapped the helpless little guy.

9/6 - Friday

Jay's two-week check up went well. We had more questions than we thought, after the exam got going. We like the pediatrician we saw, agree with her on almost everything she talked about, and found most of the information and advice very helpful.

9/7 - Saturday

As I'm talking to Jim about perhaps using some of his 52 days of sick leave beginning in October, he casually mentions that perhaps sick days are only meant to be used when the baby is sick....

Grandma Z. and Aunt Kathy showed up by 2 — of course, Jay is asleep for 2+ hours. When he's not sleeping, he's eating and going back to sleep, so they rave about what a good baby he is. By the end of the evening, however, he has barfed on both of them. He is wide awake until well after 9 and we offer only water after formula.

9/8 - Sunday

Jay awoke for a quick and ravenous midnight feeding, then slept until 3, then slept until 6! Boy, if this could happen *every* night!

Aunt Kathy and Grandma came back from their motel and cooed at him until 11 or so. I have underestimated the interest generated by a new — and relatively rare (since our family is small) — member of the family.

I got very depressed tonight about Jim going back to work and me not feeling up to par, plus the sick leave concern, and I cried for 45+ minutes. Is this more than "baby blues" and are there drugs for it?

Carpal tunnel, hemorrhoids, lochia, tired, slow, incision pain, can't lift Jay well, can't carry him around well because of surgery and my back (low-back pain). Bowels still not right, either.

9/9 - Monday

Attended our first MELD (formerly Minnesota Early Learning Design) meeting with Jay. It's basically support and information-sharing for new parents. I talked about feeling panicked when Jim goes back to work and I am alone with the baby, not feeling great and not feeling confident. One woman, also a c-section mom, said she had felt the same way. Another said she panicked when her husband went back to work after two weeks and she wasn't even a c-section. "You make it through, one diaper change at a time," she said.

The doctor said I was healing fine. He made a point of showing me how "usually we do a symmetrical incision, like a smile," but because Jay was more than 8 pounds, I got an extra inch on one side. (Funny, I hadn't noticed. Must have been busy with something else, like a new baby and healing up.)

Jay is barfing less but crying more. Perhaps he is able to keep down more gas? He screams at diaper changes — he just doesn't like to be on his back. The all-out screaming is very hard for me to take, whether or not I am the one changing the diaper.

9/11 - Wednesday

Jay's face looks broader. The infant acne on his cheeks is gone and so are the tiny whiteheads around his nose (for 13 years?). He is looking like a different kid sometimes. Growing so fast it's almost scary.

After Jim came home I took the dog in the car and went to the drug and grocery store for the first time by myself. Other than walking slower, it was just like the old days. But by 7, when it was time to go to meet some friends with their new baby on a layover at the airport, I was too bushed — that's my nap time. How depressing — I felt almost good as new, and then I'm not. I wore tennis shoes for the first time in, what, four months? They just don't have the support the Birkenstocks do and my legs ached.

Wolfed down a BLT Jim made. We traded off feeding Jay while the other one ate. When will we have a dinner together again?

9/12 - Thursday

There is this drooping house-plant I kept meaning to get watered, but it took six hours. No lie. I'd see it every time I sat down with Jay, but it took six hours to get to it. I took my shower at about 3:30 p.m., after Jim came home (he didn't get to take one this a.m., either). I will never get to shave my legs or cut my toe nails again. Jay does sleep for 90 minutes or two hours at a time, but that time seems to be taken up starting dinner, doing laundry, or little incidentals like going to the bathroom. He started crying right when I'd made lunch, so I ate at 2:30.

Our day: Up at 9:30. Jim left for work at 10. Baby cries 10:01. Make bottle, feed, burp, feed, burp, change, burp, comfort, give rest of bottle. Baby sleeps, 11:30. Baby up, 1:15. Repeat above routine. Baby up 3 p.m. or so. Repeat above. Jim home 3:30. Take shower, get out of PJs. Walk around block for first time with dog and baby in stroller, 4:30-ish. Show baby to admiring neighbors. Feel proud. Baby falls asleep. I take nap, 6. Get up, 7:30. Feed baby (see above, though shared with Jim). Hastily and ravenously eat two pieces of Jim's pizza, tomatoes and cake. Baby asleep, 9:30. Write thank-you notes. Get baby up, 10:30. Feed baby (see above). Try to keep baby awake, but fail by 11:30. Prepare bottles, refrigerate. Do dishes, clean kitchen. Watch Letterman, 12:05. Baby up, 1:30 (see above). Baby down, 2:22. Mom down after that. (Jim has post-3 a.m. shift, so he has slept through several hours of this.)

Switched Jay to disposable nurser system to reduce gas/spit-up. Took him only two bottles to get the hang of it (the doctor said it might take two-three days). He made a yucky face at first and couldn't figure out how to suck it — "nipple confusion." Then chowed down. It's true about him getting less gas.

9/13 - Friday

Got up to find Jim had had trouble with the new nipples (Jay sort of fights them) last night so he'd switched back to the old ones. We agreed to give new ones a shot until Saturday p.m. or Sunday a.m.

I felt overwhelmed today. Didn't get a shower at all. House seems messy. I have a list of things I haven't gotten done. Started calling about day care half-time, beginning in October. There are two women who do it nearby and neither will commit. Another woman, again, said that classifies as full-time, which would cost $130 a week, whether he's there four hours a day or eight.

Jim and I talked a long time about my trouble adjusting, how Jim has had virtually no trouble adjusting (which makes me really mad), and how Jay will need fuller-time day care — maybe six hours a day — sometime, but how soon? We decided Jim would try to take off October without pay and we'll use savings to make up his salary. That will help me get back to my clients' work and buy all three of us some time, plus Jim will be the best care provider around.

9/14 - Saturday

Jim gave me a great present — five hours out with a friend who's here from Washington. We did a Twin Cities driving tour and had lunch out. I drove her places I hadn't been in years and it was fun, and I came home refreshed.

We switched back to the old-fashioned nipples/bottles in the morning, as Jay seemed stressed on the disposables. But after quickly drinking four ounces, with three burps and barfing up the last ounce, we agreed to switch back. He had not forgotten the disposable nipple and did fine with it tonight.

The kid is growing like crazy. He's almost outgrown his small bassinet, and I dressed him in a medium-sized jumpsuit thing tonight, which is only a little too big.

Jim said Jay slept only about a half-hour while I was gone, so maybe he is getting to know days vs. nights and will sleep longer than two hours at night.

9/15 - Sunday

Jay was, indeed, quite awake most of the 11 a.m. -3 p.m. stretch, then some this evening. He drank nearly six ounces at 10 p.m., so we'll see how long that keeps him asleep.

Other than my mom and my sister, we had our first babysitters tonight. Barb and Glen, the neighbors who love babies, kept him while we went to a movie. It wasn't particularly hard to leave him, but about half-way through the movie I sort of missed him, like I wanted to lean over his bassinet and check him, or that he should be with us. He was fine, of course, when we picked him up, and didn't miss me a bit. It felt good to hold Jay again, though. (He peed on Barb's work calendar. "It'll dry," she said. What a trooper!)

The new disposable bottles — second time — seem to present no problem to him now.

Maxine came over and fed Jay and held him. It has really surprised me how much people like babies, even other people's babies (I never did).

9/16 - Monday

Jay has changed. His eyes, mostly. They don't lock on to you by accident. They seek you out and follow you. His arms are still wildly — embarrassingly, almost, for such a mature baby! — uncontrolled, but not as erratic, somehow. He is awake more, so there are more opportunities to "communicate" with him. Still no smiles, but he's working on it.

We borrowed a baby bath tub from the neighbors and Jay had his first bath in it in the kitchen sink. Hated it. Screamed the whole time, which probably was two or three minutes. At the very end, the screaming turned to sobbing, like he was breaking down and falling completely apart, which he's never done before and which just tore at my little mommy heartstrings. Jim said later he didn't even notice it. We rarely let this kid cry for long — I just can't stand it — which is why we headed home after a shopping trip to the discount store. He woke up, wanted a bottle and was trapped in his car seat on his back, not our little boy's favorite position.

9/17 - Tuesday

The minute Jim left today I stepped in the shower and the minute I stepped out this baby started to cry. He was mostly awake for the next four hours, which doesn't seem like much when I write it down, but is an eternity in terms of 10-minute intervals, which was about as long as he wanted to be in his chair, or rocked, or fed/burped, or in his stroller outdoors, or as long as I wanted to carry him around the house.

Jim goes back to work full-time tomorrow, and it is only today I felt confident about handling the baby. Only experience does it. It's really scary, for example, when Jay gulps too fast and chokes. But his little esophageal system handles it. I tip him up on my shoulder ASAP and pat his back, and he hasn't died yet, knock on wood. I notice I am flinging him around to take a bottle, for instance, almost one-handed, no small feat with braces for the carpal tunnel. I don't get so panicked when he cries. Some of it is I am feeling so much more normal — I can take the stairs almost as fast as before surgery.

9/18 - Wednesday

First full day of baby care, alone, went fine. In fact, I noticed some new stuff about my son. For instance, he now has this endearing quality, when he falls asleep on my chest, of draping one little baby arm over my arm. Of course, I know that arm wasn't *placed* there, that it just fell into position partly because it had no where else to go. But it *looks* as if he has tried to put his arm around me and give me a hug.

Jay is either wanting to be held more or he is heavier and I am noticing it more. It's probably because he's awake more without eating.

This baby is growing eyelashes. Maybe he always had them, but they are really noticeable now.

Today, during a happy diaper change, I got to get most of the lint out from between his fingers. His nails, however, still look like he is pursuing certification as a master gardener. I can't figure out how they get so dirty when he can't move or go anywhere.

For some odd reason, I assumed little babies, unless they were crying, were quiet. Our guy has quite a repertoire of grunts and groans and coos. They've gotten louder as he's gotten older. The most shockingly loud are the groans when I lift him to my shoulder for a burp — he groans as if he were lifting all 12 pounds of him himself — especially if there is discomfort-causing gas in there (and there always is). He grunts and stretches his entire body out when he poops, even though constipation is not a problem. The coos that emanate from his crib or when he settles contentedly on my chest are genuinely "awwww!"-inspiring.

9/19 - Thursday

I woke up at 7:30, tired, and this baby didn't go back to sleep for more than 15 minutes without fussing. All day. Sometimes so badly that I'd pick him up from his bassinet. Jim and I both agreed he does cry more. But it's usually for a reason, and most often that's because he wants more bottle.

This may have been only my second day of full-time baby care, but it was enough to know I'd better get day care lined up. And I am not a candidate for staying home myself. By 4 or 4:30, I found myself desensitized to more crying, and I let him sit in his chair and cry while making a bottle, rather than picking him up and doing it one-handed. I am not saying the nurse in the hospital nursery with the wind-up swing was right, but I guess I can understand why one more crying newborn didn't faze her.

Our second attempt at a bath went better — Jay didn't cry until a few minutes into it. (Perhaps I had the bath water too hot the other night? Who knows?)

9/20 - Friday
Took a "long" stroller ride when Jay had a fairly full stomach. He cried four times but was consolable by picking up. After the fourth time he went to sleep.

Jim went out of town so I had Jay and the dog alone from 9 a.m. to 7 p.m. (Jim was practically itching to hold him when he got home. The baby, not the dog.) I experimented once at about 11:30 a.m. with the "let cry" theory for fussiness. All that did, near as I can tell, was wind him up more. Since nothing seemed to calm him — a bottle, the stovehood fan, rocking, burping, watching the chandelier at diaper change, singing, change of scenery — I resorted to his first automatic swing "ride." He looked angry, like, "You put me in here and I can't do anything about it because I can't control my arms and legs, but I'm not pleased." Then he fell asleep.

I made myself a new rule on the fussiness — since most of the time he's just plain hungry, I will feed him as much as he wants when he wants it, as long as he doesn't barf from overfeeding. (He hasn't done that in a long time, due to disposable nursers.) I figure his needs are pretty simple and he's too young to say he wants it, but not really mean it, or have some eating disorder. Besides, he did refuse the bottle today when hunger wasn't the issue.

9/21 - Saturday
Jim let me sleep in until nearly 9:30 — heaven!

Jim and I disagree on the when-to-feed issue. He thinks Jay is often bored and just needs stimulation and Jim doesn't have a problem making Jay wait for it. I figure, why screw around and upset him, when he's rooting and fussy and a bottle is what he wants, why not give it to him?

I do agree on the stimulation issue, though. Now that he is less gassy and very comfortable on his back, it's easier to do more with him. Jim put a mirror in his crib and I set up a "crib gym."

We joined the neighbors and their two kids at Fuddrucker's for Jay's first restaurant. He slept in his car seat through most of it. There were at least two other babies in car seats and many other kids there, and it's noisy so no one cares much if they scream.

9/22 - Sunday

Today was Jay's shower from some neighbors. Two other babies, six and three months, were there, and it was helpful to compare parenting notes. His movement from wonderful, eat-and-sleep baby to fussy-12-pound-slavemaster will pass, they said, into a wonderful stage where he will be less fussy, can sit happily by himself, grin, be easily entertained and, possibly, sleep through the night.

Some of that, of course, is going on now. I think he has begun to smile, sort of, and, man, was he wide awake today. Slept for intermittent periods of a half hour or so all day except for one major three hour nap. Even the stove hood fan only kept him enraptured for short periods. It is fun, though, when he's wide awake and paying attention only to *you* and locks eyes only with *you*, the greatest thing in his world.

9/23 - Monday

Jay was really fussy about taking the nipple at his 12:30 a.m. feeding and I got up to find he had struggled against it for 50 minutes with Jim at 4 a.m. Jim switched back to the old, regular nipples and said Jay relaxed immediately, drank and fell asleep. I called the pediatrician, and a nurse called back and said not to worry about his mouth/tongue development switching nipples yet again. So we are going back to the old bottles and nipples.

I have my first editorial meeting with a client on Wednesday, Jim will be at a Twins game from 6-10 p.m. the Tuesday night before, so I'm a little concerned about finding work clothes I can fit into and getting them washed, dried and ironed, for instance, let alone prepare material.

This afternoon, when he was up, we "played" with the play "gym," which has little plastic characters that hang over him about 8 inches away. He looked and looked and batted his arms and kicked his legs, all excited. Sometimes now, we see little smiles. They don't always make sense — we woke him up to go to a MELD meeting, and he sat in his car seat and smiled — but they're always an occasion to call the other parent.

Tonight at the meeting we talked about fathering, and one facilitator commented on how her husband is better at playing with their three kids than she. She said she had to learn to join in. "Otherwise, it's no fun" doing the behind-the-scenes infrastructure work that is invisible to children, she said. I, too, will have to learn from Jim how to play more, even at this stage.

9/24 - Tuesday

Jay is officially one month old today. Boy, the changes — physical, yes, but developmental, too. He weighs 12 or 13 pounds, has grown nearly two inches. His whole body, of course, is bigger, but it's his head I notice most (because it's uncovered? Because it has a face and gets looked at??) and his face is broader, more defined.

Sometimes, now with his well-focused eyes and his more controlled facial expressions, I see him as a more mature child-person, trapped in an uncontrolled, immature, non-verbal baby body. He seems to know what he wants (nine times out of 10, food), and what he doesn't want (the pacifier, for example), but can't communicate other than crying or grunting or cooing or flailing his arms and legs. I believe he has baby dreams, and there's certainly some primitive sense of humor (sometimes it seems he just smiles because he feels good — full tummy, rested, dry, clean, warm, lack of gas. Would that we all be so happy just for lack of physical discomfort!).

I am so much more comfortable with taking care of him. He's not so fragile and he doesn't "break," yet he is not so complicated that, to date, I've only once not been able to figure out what's bugging him. (Knock on wood that he not become colicky — surely it would undermine any parental confidence.)

He can be demanding. Today I made a number of calls to try to arrange half-time day care (which no providers with experience seem to want to do), starting in November (he will be about 10 weeks old..), with no luck. Is he *too* demanding so that no one wants to care for our baby? I will try not to take it so personally.

He may be only a month old, but in some ways it seems he has been with us forever. I can still remember going to bed at 10 p.m. or so and not getting up until 7 or 8. And getting care for him so that I can go to my business meeting tomorrow (Jim will take him to work) is an inconvenience, no doubt (it will be the first time since his birth I have been in the car without the dog, Jim or Jay, or some combination thereof). But he is such a focus for us. I can remember thinking after Kirby was out of puppyhood and knew the rules and routines around here, how life without Kirby would be so unusual, how she was just such a part of our lives. With a little human, childhood will continue to throw challenges as growth takes so much longer than the one year of puppyhood. But Jay will become so much a part of all of us, too. He is a member of the family. We have made it through a month, we will make it a lifetime.

146

Index

About the Author

Laura Zahn (shown here with her new neighbor, Kyle Koppy, age 2 1/2 weeks) is a St. Paul, Minnesota, writer who researched this book while she was pregnant with her first child, then re-wrote it after her baby was born. She has worked in journalism and public relations in Alaska and Minnesota and founded the publishing company, Down to Earth Publications. She publishes the popular regional Bed & Breakfast cookbook series, "WAKE UP AND SMELL THE COFFEE." (Photo by Jim Miller)